MALTA REMEMBERED

First edition
published in 2005 by

WOODFIELD PUBLISHING
Bognor Regis, West Sussex, England
www.woodfieldpublishing.com

ISBN 1-903953-94-4

MALTA
Remembered

By Those Who Were There
During World War Two

EDITED BY
FRANK RIXON BEM

Woodfield

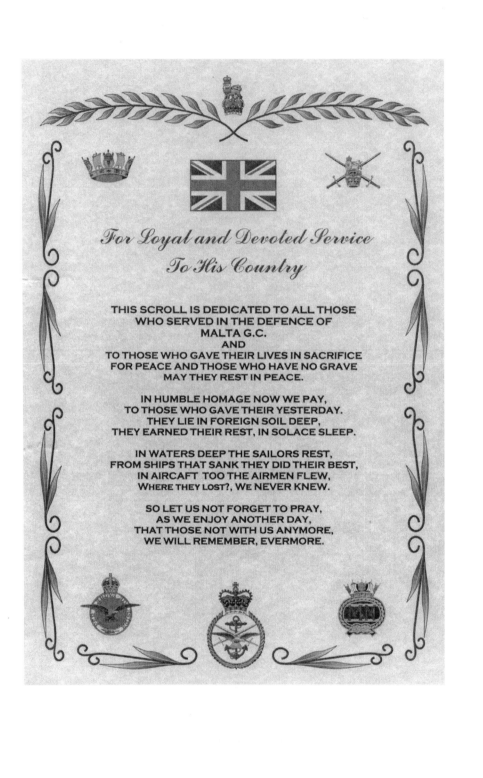

For Loyal and Devoted Service
To His Country

THIS SCROLL IS DEDICATED TO ALL THOSE
WHO SERVED IN THE DEFENCE OF
MALTA G.C.
AND
TO THOSE WHO GAVE THEIR LIVES IN SACRIFICE
FOR PEACE AND THOSE WHO HAVE NO GRAVE
MAY THEY REST IN PEACE.

IN HUMBLE HOMAGE NOW WE PAY,
TO THOSE WHO GAVE THEIR YESTERDAY.
THEY LIE IN FOREIGN SOIL DEEP,
THEY EARNED THEIR REST, IN SOLACE SLEEP.

IN WATERS DEEP THE SAILORS REST,
FROM SHIPS THAT SANK THEY DID THEIR BEST,
IN AIRCAFT TOO THE AIRMEN FLEW,
WHERE THEY LOST?, WE NEVER KNEW.

SO LET US NOT FORGET TO PRAY,
AS WE ENJOY ANOTHER DAY,
THAT THOSE NOT WITH US ANYMORE,
WE WILL REMEMBER, EVERMORE.

Contents

Foreword by HRH Prince Philip

My only connection with Malta during the war was a very short visit to pick up a few stores while serving in HMS Wallace. We were on our way to take part in the Allied landings on Sicily in 1942. The visit was quite long enough for me to get a vivid impression of the devastating damage caused by enemy bombing. The physical damage was obvious enough, but it gave little indication of what life must have been like for the civilian population, or for the members of the British Services, who were engaged in the stubborn defence of the island.

Malta has a long history of warfare and sieges, but it is the stories of individuals that bring history to life. 'Malta Remembered' contains a collection of remarkable accounts by individuals, who fought on, from and over the island, and who lived to tell their tales. This has ensured that the human experience of the 20th century Siege is recorded for posterity.

I am sure that anyone with a general interest in the history of the Second World War will be impressed by these detailed accounts, and this 'source material' will certainly be most valuable for future historians. I hope it will also be read by the descendents of the authors, and by those who had friends and relations serving in Malta during the war. It is a tribute to their dedicated service.

Philip

About the Editor

Frank Rixon was born at Padworth, Berkshire, the son of a carter who had also been a soldier. On the death of his mother he was sent to St Edward's Home in Huntingdon and later to St Augustine's home in Sevenoaks, Kent. At the age of 14 years 3 months he enlisted as a Band Boy in the 2nd Battalion of the Queen's Own Royal West Kent Regiment at Shornecliffe on 1 shilling per day. In 1936 he was posted to India to join the Regiment's 1st Battalion in Trimulgherry and later Karachi.

He returned to the UK in 1938 but on the outbreak of World War 2 was posted to the RASC at Luton until his sister signed consent forms, after which he was posted to join the 2nd Battalion of the West Kents in Malta, where he stayed throughout the Siege. The Battalion was posted to Egypt in 1943 and then to the Dodecanese Islands of Samos and Kos. After the fall of Leros Frank escaped down the Turkish coast in a minesweeper, travelling by night and hiding under cliffs by day, eventually returning to Egypt.

After a spell training newcomers from the UK he was posted home to Maidstone, Kent, with what was left of the battalion, and later to 164 Officers Training Unit at Barmouth, thence to Chester and finally Trentham Park, Staffordshire. On return to his depot there was a posting to train National Servicemen at 2 Training Bn REME at Honiton, Devon.

He transferred to REME in 1952 and was posted to 16 Britcom Infantry Workshops in Korea and thence, after 18 months, to 40 Base Workshops, Singapore, where he was awarded the British Empire Medal (BEM). He returned to the UK in 1955 to 3 Training Battalion REME at Arbourfield, Berks, where he retired in 1957 as a Warrant Officer Class 2 after 22 years service.

After a short spell in other jobs there was a chance to join the Civil Service as a Barrack Accountant and later he was promoted to Civilian Accommodation Officer. After 24 years he retired in 1986. He has since held several offices with the George Cross Island Association.

Acknowledgements

My most grateful thanks to all those who have contributed to the stories and photographs in this book and which without their efforts by keeping diaries etc; this book could never have been written, To my daughter Sarah, my Granddaughter Diane and to my Grandson Dominic whose has assisted in typing out the stories. To Colin Randall who on the death of his mother his father's old wartime album was found and he kindly loaned me this for the stories and the photographs therein. This book is dedicated in the memory of all those who served in the defence of Malta G.C.

Frank Rixon, 2005

1. THE SIEGE OF MALTA

War did not come actively to the Mediterranean area until after Italy entered the war on 10th June 1940. Malta then became of great strategic importance as the bases from which Allied Forces could attack enemy facilities and lines of communication between Italy and North Africa. Had Malta fallen the German Army might not have outrun its supplies at El Alamein, Cairo might have been captured and with it the Suez Canal. The way then would have been open to the Gulf oil wells and history might have been fundamentally changed. Twice in 1942 Malta was within days of surrender from starvation.

The Royal Navy had the task of striking whenever possible at enemy shipping ferrying troops and materials from Italy to North Africa. They also provided escorts for vital Allied convoys through the Mediterranean, from Gibraltar in the east to Alexandria in the west. They played a particularly vital role as far as Malta was concerned, ferrying aircraft and ammunition and escorting the merchant convoys of supplies without which the island could not have held out against the enemy.

Smaller vessels and submarines also played a very prominent role in attacking enemy shipping and carrying supplies and paid a heavy price in the loss of gallant ships and personnel.

At the outset there were only 4,000 British Army troops on the island but later this was reinforced to 30,000 with a third being Maltese. The infantry unloaded ships, built pens to protect aircraft, constructed and manned defence posts all around the island and manned anti-aircraft positions on the airfields. In fact they undertook any type of work, including helping the RAF to maintain, re-arm and re-fuel their aircraft. They also helped with bomb-loading on aircraft such as Wellingtons. They built runways at Hal Far (mainly Fleet Air Arm) Luqa and Ta'kali, with a long strip at Safi for dispersing aircraft, and helped to maintain them after repeated enemy bombing attacks, which was just as vital to our success as the work carried out by the aircraft, which could not have taken off otherwise. The Royal Artillery played a vital role in defending the island; manning the guns for hours on end with very little sleep whilst being targeted by the fighters and bombers of the Axis.

The contribution of the Royal Air Force to the defence of the island was of utmost importance. Most of the RAF aircrews on Malta were British, but there were also a significant number from our Commonwealth allies. They flew at first Gladiators and Swordfish, then Hurricanes, Spitfires, Wellingtons, Beaufighters and sundry other aircraft in the face of overwhelming superiority (in numbers) of the German and Italian air forces.

Airfields across the island were badly hit and the maintenance of aircraft must have been a nightmare; the shortage of spares and the destruction of other supplies testing the ingenuity of ground crews to the limit; but they did not fail. The turn of the tide came with the arrival of Spitfires from the USS *Wasp*, CV7 and HMS *Eagle* in May 1942, thanks to which the island regained air superiority.

The local population were caught up in a horrifying war situation that was not of their making, but they stoically and bravely came to support the Allied forces in many ways. Under intense aerial bombardment they unloaded ships, which ensured that the island could be fed and that the armed forces would receive the ammunition and stores they needed to hold out against and strike back at the enemy. Rations were very meagre indeed and it was a miracle that they could sustain the devotion and courage required to carry out the many tasks allotted to them. But this they did, and in recognition of the fact on the 15th April 1942 King George VI awarded the island a unique accolade, the George Cross, normally given to individual civilians who have displayed acts of uncommon valour, but on this occasion awarded to the entire island – an honour never bestowed before or since– and to this day the insignia is proudly depicted on the Maltese flag.

The contribution of the Merchant Navy must also be given full recognition. Time after time convoys entered the Mediterranean to fight their way through to Malta and the price they paid was very heavy indeed, with many a good ship and its crewmembers lost in a holocaust of bombardment from enemy aircraft and motor torpedo boats. Possibly the most famous convoy was the 'Pedestal' Convoy of 1942, which against all odds and supported by the largest naval force ever assembled, fought through against repeated enemy attacks to bring relief to the island and its defenders. In particular the tanker *Ohio* carried essential fuel to keep the island going.

THE COST

During the Siege of Malta the following lives were lost:
1,600 Maltese Civilians, 200 Merchant Navy personnel, 1,700 submariners, 2,200 other RN personnel, 700 Army personnel, 900 RAF personnel.

Over 10,000 domestic and commercial buildings were damaged or destroyed and had to be rebuilt, likewise 100 Government buildings, churches, hospitals, etc.

To keep Malta supplied 118 British and Allied merchant vessels were escorted by 11 battleships, 2 battle cruisers, 9 aircraft carriers, 40 cruisers, 3 fast mine layers 154 destroyers and over 90 other craft; 91 submarines patrolled in support.

Of these the following ships were lost: 14 merchant vessels, 2 aircraft carriers, 4 cruisers, 1 fast mine layer, 18 destroyers, 40 submarines and 23 other craft. Many other ships were so badly damaged so that they needed long periods to be repaired. This will give the readers some idea of the cost of defending the little island of Malta GC.

Overlooking the bomb damaged homes near the harbour in Valletta

Children playing in the bomb damaged Valletta

Men of the RAF walking through the bomb damaged streets of Valletta

2.   THE EARLY DAYS

Joseph C. Bushell - 16th Fortress Company Royal Engineers

In Malta before World War II started there were two permanently stationed regular units of the Royal Engineers, with clearly defined roles to play in the defence of the island. 16th Fortress Company was responsible for anti-aircraft searchlight duties, whilst 24th Fortress Company had coastal defence, including searchlights and later on provided the Bomb Disposal Unit, a job they learned as they went along.

March 1939 saw me arrive to join 16th Company (Searchlights) having been trained at Haslar Barracks, Gosport. Much of the time was spent on training at night with the help of Swordfish aircraft flying from Hal Far. On occasions we were given the opportunity to fly at night in the "target" planes to see what the searchlights looked like at the other end.

Of course these were halcyon days and I do not think that many young people at the time could see the possibility of war. It was the days of the "Gut" and the "Gharry" with Housey-Housey at the Vernon and La Valette Clubs, Grand Opera at the Opera House in Strada Reale, chicken and chips for half a crown and Blue Label beer at three pence a bottle. (When the declaration of war against Germany came I was, in fact, manning a searchlight on Hal Far 'drome.) The pace of life did not change that much and there was plenty of everything; war still seemed a long way away.

Early in 1940 it was decided to move the detachment from Hal Far to a coastal position about a mile from the Grand Harbour in the direction of Kalafrana. It was an old Victorian coastal fort. In the walls of the main emplacement there were still embedded huge steel rings which one supposed were used to move a single gun.

Our war really started on 10th June 1940, when Italy declared war that evening. The following day the bombing started and it was all rather different to what one imagined. The raids continued on and off all day, with, of course, the attendant rumours: so many planes had been shot down – so many people had been killed – we were going to be invaded – and so forth.

At about six that night we were told that yet another raid was approaching the Grand Harbour and this time the bombers could be seen. The target was obviously the Grand Harbour itself; bombs fell into the sea at the approach to the harbour and on land between us and the nearest coastal defence battery at St Rocco. At this time three launches from St Angelo were returning to Grand Harbour, having been out trying to salvage an Italian merchant vessel that had attempted to scuttle off the coast. Amid the bombing and confusion we were rather surprised when the battery at St Rocco opened fire on these launches.

We thought that we were being invaded and that they must be Italians, a view falsely confirmed when one after the other the launches were blown out of the water and firing was also taken up by beach defence positions. Sadly, it was later confirmed by survivors reaching the shore that the launches were, in fact, R.N.

SHALL WE DANCE?

Christmas 1942 found me as 2 i/c of a searchlight detachment on a hill overlooking Sliema and Manoel Island. In some strange fashion it emerged that out of 11 men in the detachment there were 7 who did not know how to dance in a 'proper' manner. It also emerged that one of the number knew a "female impersonator" who lived in Floriana, in fact before the war there were some well known persons of this calling. Such names come to mind as "Sugar" "Chris" "Vicky" and "Bobby". Well our chap knew "Chris" and it was agreed that "Chris" would come to our detachment once a week where, for the sum of two shillings, he would give dancing lessons to the seven. This was taken very seriously but there were a few snags. One, our mess room was in fact an old barn. Two, it was a dirt floor. Three, December and January were wet months and the barn floor tended to muddy during the two hours or so of dancing. On one occasion we had to wear 'wellies". Four, the music was provided by an old wind-up gramophone on which the spring was weak and it tended to run down during the session. Fifth and last, we had only one record, a slow foxtrot entitled "My Heart Belongs to Daddy".

As a result, at the end of the war our seven would-be Fred Astairs went home but later, when married, could only manage to dance if the band could be persuaded to play this tune!

3. SCOUTING IN WARTIME MALTA

Ronald Walford - 1st Tigne (National Service) Troop

Just imagine what a purple-faced Regimental Sergeant-Major might have said had anyone told him that right in the middle of a heavy shooting War he'd be expected to issue orders to a mob of little kiddywinkies – no naughty cuss-words 'cause Mummy won't like it if little Billy comes home with a mouthful of Army slang – all orders to be put gently in case some tiny tot bursts into tears – it's complications like that which make it so remarkable that even the most junior Scouts played a part in the Siege of Malta, a part which led to the award of the Scout Bronze Medal to the Malta Scout Association. Yet it makes sense if one looks at the history of scouting in Malta.

The full story is told in John Mizzi's remarkable book *Scouting in Malta: an Illustrated History*. John tells how Malta was the second country in the world to establish a Scout Association (on 9th November 1908) after Baden-Powell set up the Scouts in England just a few months earlier. That quick start arose because Baden-Powell knew Malta well; he had been the Assistant Military Secretary there from 1890 to 1893. His family already had service connections with the Malta zone and by all accounts B-P settled in quickly and soon established a reputation for being something of a party animal. After serving happily in Malta he became famous for his defence of Mafeking during the Boer War, from which he returned to England to found the Scouts.

From the beginning, Maltese children played the major part in the Scout Troops. Although many children of UK servicemen joined, most Troops were completely Maltese and the rest a mix of UK and Maltese. This mixing continued happily until the events of 1940-43 made it difficult, to say the least, for youngsters to travel to Scout meetings. It was then that Troops became narrowly localised, with a split between UK children in barracks forming their own Troops and Maltese children continuing with whatever Troop they could reach without straying too far from home.

When it came to war service the senior Scouts immediately offered their services and some new Troops were set up specifically to help the war effort. So what did we do? First, all those Scouts engaged in war work hoisted the National Service emblem – a bright red bar emblazoned in gold with the letters NS. This highly-prized badge meant that a Scout was eligible for suitable war work, with that work being allocated almost always on the basis of age. Older Scouts became virtual servicemen, working alongside Regulars in many tasks. The 12 to 15 year-olds busied themselves with various fairly harmless jobs and tiny Cubs and Brownies – well, they just got under people's feet and compensated for this by being terribly enthusiastic.

As was usual in wartime Malta, the shortage of paper meant that few records were kept, and even those were lost when the Scout Headquarters were destroyed on April 7th 1942 – that famously bad month for the whole Island. But we do know for certain that many Scouts joined the supposedly adult Malta volunteer Force, with some falsifying their age to do so; the youngest recorded was 14. That meant serving as reserve soldiers, carrying rifles, working on and around gun positions and in general taking the same risks as troops and airmen. Others did good work at Naval Wireless Stations around the islands, where they helped to conduct tests, to listen out for signals, and then to collate and record them. It was tedious, but it released men for more active duties and as such it received formal congratulations from the Navy. We also know that some Sea Scouts worked in the Castile but in spite of many efforts we can't trace who they were or exactly what they did.

Another valuable task made good use of our excellent young eyesight we spotted four aircraft and found that we could not only see them but count their engines and identify high-flying Savoia Marchettis and Capronis. Not just spotting, by the way, but the accurate measurement and reporting of ranges and bearings. Coastal spotting came our way but with less to see apart from the horizon-hugging Axis rescue floatplanes. Then, when a convoy arrived, senior Scouts helped to unload ships. It proved a difficult and sometimes dangerous task because of the existence of a black market and the need to keep a close eye on valuable food stores. One Scout remembers how he and others, in full Scout uniform and armed with staves, sat in the backs of trucks to fend off certain types trying to help food to 'fall off the back of the lorry'. Again, formal thanks were expressed for the good work done and for the utter reliability of these sometimes quite young Scouts.

The heavy bombing damaged the telephone system so badly that many military groups turned to the Scouts for help with carrying messages. One can't pretend that these messages were of world-shattering military importance, but the transfer of much of the routine signals work to Scouts relieved the strain on the proper system, so keeping it clear for urgent traffic. Scouts of all ages trotted around happily, carrying Station Daily Orders, shopping lists for the NAAFI wagon, 'send-three-and-fourpence-going-to-a-dance' style messages and indeed the whole variety of everyday communications without which no service can function. A snag with message-carrying was that tiny junior Scouts couldn't wear tin hats; if we had done so we wouldn't have seen where we were going and might have frightened the life out of sentries confronted by apparently self-propelled headgear shuffling along the ground. In the absence of protective helmets we were ordered to take cover during AA gunfire, an instruction most of us ignored, not because we were dashed brave young chaps but because to do so was boring – until the shrapnel came too close, whereupon we broke all records in the rush to safety!

Senior types took over routine guard duties, mainly around gun sites and remotely-located military gear such as searchlights and predictors. A few Scouts were told off to watch out for spies without being enlightened as to what a spy might look like. (Sinister types in swirling black cloaks carrying parcels labelled Bomb?) That was what our comics showed, so that's who we looked for and failed to find. Rather more useful was the training given to seniors in First Aid and general rescue work.

We also reported the location of unexploded bombs and the larger bits of downed aircraft. At least, we were meant to, but no self-respecting youngster with any sense of adventure will surrender a treasure like a bomb to the authorities without doing some kind of gingerly-conducted experiments; several of us came near to Heaven, in both senses, during our examination of bomb casings which had broken open on impact to display the fascinating store of TNT inside – a surprisingly inert substance, we found.

In all these activities what counted most, and what seems to have impressed our elders most, was the keenness and dedication of Scouts. Of course Scouts were unpaid (a few were given a tiny allowance) and didn't receive any favourable treatment when it came to rations and so on, but these were small matters which no Scout worried about. Instead it was just the knowledge that one was taking part in a mixture of a glorious game and a deadly real war which accounted for the zest and enthusiasm which propelled us.

In September 1942 Lord Gort presented the George Cross to the Islands. A few months later, in May 1943, he made another presentation, this time to the Malta Scout Association, of the Scout Bronze Medal, awarded us by the London HQ. Years later the founding of the GCIA led to the striking of the George Cross Commemoration Medal, which, for some reason, Scouts are not eligible to receive. So the Malta Scout Association, in a typically generous move, went to enormous trouble to contact those overseas Scouts who had served in Malta during the Siege to award them a replica of our Bronze Medal – the little red ribbon and bronze medallion you'll see on the right lapel of Scouts at George Cross Island Association meetings. It can't compete with the huge range of gallantry and campaign medals sported by adult members of the G.C.I.A, but then we Scouts never considered ourselves to be in that same league, and we were happy that. We had done something to help and had followed the standards set by our Founder, B-P himself, in the very islands where he had spent so much time. To us it seemed completely appropriate that we had won our spurs in a siege which echoed the famous Siege of Mafeking where B-P had first found fame.

4. LUQA AND THOSE WHO SERVED THERE

L.A.C Dick Francis - RAF

My memories of life on Malta began at Wilmslow, (NO.G.P.D.C.) where we began to assemble for a journey which took us to Malta. My kitbag, which I still have, bore the legend "Raffles" which suggests our original destination may have been Singapore.

It was at Wilmslow where I first came across three airmen who became lifelong friends: Joe Forth, Fred Foster and Frank Moran. Alas, they are no longer with us. It has been tragic to see such stalwarts fade away and die. We were all wireless operators who, at Luqa, carried out duties as wireless mechanics.

In those days Joe Forth would be remembered as a strong and fearless airman who carried out his duties with complete disregard for enemy action. Fred Foster, a brilliant pianist, entertained everybody in the old wooden NAAFI building. Later he played classical music in the British Institute and at times was heard on the Maltese Rediffusion Service. Some may remember that he played piano at the Bulls Head at Handfort (near Wilmslow) where the landlady (of blessed memory) fed us on fried steak sandwiches and treated us to packets of cigarettes, which she concealed under her apron. (We paid a post-war visit to her pub and she greeted us with much pleasure.) Frank Moran was another conscientious airman and a devout Roman Catholic. He rarely missed going to Mass on Sunday, mainly in Quormi, whatever the state of play.

Our next port of call on board the *Leinster* was Gibraltar, where through a porthole we saw a brilliantly-lit dockside in sharp contrast to the blackout at home. We were forbidden to go on deck during daylight because of watchful eyes on the Spanish mainland.

We departed Gibraltar in darkness, under a cover of dense mist coming down off the rock. Sounds of drink-inspired revelry came from the crew's quarters (I think they had been allowed shore leave). Otherwise everything was quite ghostly. I had been nominated duty signaller and, armed with an Aldis Lamp (totally ineffective because of the thick fog) I remained on deck accompanied by a naval person. We chugged along slowly for some time before we heard an almighty crash. The matelot shouted: "We've run aground!" and dashed off. I ran down to 'D' Deck to alert my sleeping comrades but they didn't want to know and told me where to go – whereupon I invited them all to drown, grabbed my small kit and returned to the top deck.

The farce that followed would have made a good comic film. Ham-fisted attempts were made to lower the lifeboats and passengers rushed to get on board, even though the Captain had ordered everybody to wait their turn. Having been on deck early I found myself on the first boat to be launched. We zig-zagged our way down to the water and it's a miracle we didn't get thrown into the sea. We then struggled to manoeuvre the long oars to push ourselves clear of the *Leinster*. Eventually all lifeboats were launched, along with a small motorboat, which then began an operation intended to tie up the lifeboats in a 'vick' made up of three on one side and four on the other. The matelot organising the procedure from the motor boat shouted his instructions in Naval language: to three lifeboats "hard a-port" and to the other four "hard a-starboard" and was totally misunderstood, with consequent loss of tempers.

The airman at the front of the first boat was asked to "pass the painter" to the motorboat but it was some time before he could be made to understand that this meant that he was required to lift a large coil of rope and pass it. When he eventually tried to lift it he found it too heavy and promptly dropped it into the water. A monocled army officer had hold of the rudder, but apparently didn't know his port from his starboard and ended up being called a "one-eyed bastard".

Little did we know that the waters around the Spanish coast (we had run aground at Terifa Point) were mined…

Daylight was breaking when a powerful British Navy motorboat came to our rescue. The Captain invited 20 of us to climb aboard (climbing a rope ladder dangling in space is no mean feat!) and we sampled a steaming mug of beautifully sweetened RN tea.

Having secured the lifeboats in line astern he then shouted to his driver "Let her go Geordie!" The motorboat shot forward at speed, causing the lifeboats to rear up and almost toss everybody into the drink.

"Five knots, not 55 knots!" roared the Captain, and we settled down to move slowly back to Gibraltar, where we subsequently bearded the French line *Pasteur* to await the rest of the *Lienster's* passengers. I have a mental picture of Flight Sergeant "Lofty" Bonsey coming aboard with all his personal possessions in a topee-bag over his shoulder on the end of a stick (a la Dick Whittington).

During the ensuing 10 days spent in Gibraltar we enjoyed excellent French food and good Scottish beer. We also witnessed the return of the naval escort to our convoy. We heard stories from the survivors of the battered ships and thanked our lucky stars we hadn't been part of the action.

Late one night we were paraded on the *Pasteur* deck and then divided into three parties. We marched with our kit (which had been rescued from the *Leinster*) down to the mole, where cruisers HMS *Arethusa* and *Hermione* and fast minelayer HMS *Manxman* awaited us, and set sail with an escort of destroyers across the Med. We were informed that HMS *Ark Royal* with Force 'H' had preceded us to create a diversion by setting fire to cork forests in Sardinia.

I was on HMS *Hermione*, where I was delighted to find that one of its crew, Stoker Frank Charnock, came from my home district and had even worked in the same factory as me (small world!). Frank instructed me in all aspects of marine life and was even kind enough to share his rum ration with me. He told me that HMS *Hermione* was on her last trip prior to returning to Blighty for a refit. Alas it didn't turn out like that. He had agreed to take home with him a letter to my fiancée and some small gifts I'd bought for her from shops on the Rock, but they, like him, ended up at the bottom of the Med on 16th June 1942, along with 82 other crew members when the Hermione was sunk by a German U-Boat (U-205).

A few years ago, having seen a notice in the *Sunday Express* about a reunion of HMS *Hermione* survivors, I wrote to their Secretary (who obviously had not been born in 1941) saying that I understood from reading Tony Spooner's *Supreme Gallantry* that HMS *Hermione* had perished with all hands. He said it had not.

Whilst on board HMS *Hermione* I was impressed by the Navy's habit of informing all on board whatever action was going on. One night, when the message "stand-by to ram" was piped, Frank advised me to grab hold of the mess deck. Good advice. Seconds later a heavy thump caused the ship to roll from side to side and we were tossed about like corks, with kitbags, tin hats, rifles and other impedimenta flying all around. A second piped message informed us that an Italian submarine had been spotted in the light path of a low moon, presumably charging its batteries. The incident was reported briefly in the *Malta Times*, a scorched copy of which is still in my possession.

The day we sailed into Grand Harbour at Malta with the Barrakka walls lined with cheering spectators has lived long in my memory. Thus began my life (and near death) for the next two or three years on Malta GC…

Our first night was spent sleeping on the floor of an office building containing filing cabinets and metal cupboards riddled with bullet holes. Quite strange! After a long cold shower we made our way to the wooden NAAFI hut, where we were delighted to find beer, "egg 'n' cheeps" and better still … a piano. Luqa hadn't had a good pianist for some time and when Fred Foster laid his magic fingers on the keys the whole place was soon singing its head off. Fred was in constant demand until an ill-directed bomb pranged both the NAAFI and the piano.

Now I come to a few vignettes of life on Luqa. I feel that readers will want to be reminded of their former comrades and so I will mention as many names as I can. I do not have an infallible memory but one name reminds me of another and so on… I am deeply indebted to the Orderly Room stalwarts Reg Frost and Bill Vernon, who produced a typed list of familiar names. I have a copy of that list and will quote from it later.

One of the characters I remember well was the larger than life Nick Nicholson from the Wireless & Armourers billet, who used to regale us with tales of his pre-war life working in the kitchens of Wormwood Scrubs. Nick was not unfamiliar with the Black Market and when ribbed about his nefarious activities would comment "Well, you've got to earn a crust!" When I later in the war met Frank Moran in Gwent (where he was working on signals) he mentioned that he had come across a signal, "requesting the whereabouts of LAC Nicholson". Nick was obviously still up to his old tricks!

Paddy Patterson and Frank Green I remember well, indeed I have a snapshot of them bathing on the rocks at Sliema, together with Phil Scholfield, Frank Moran, Freddy Pitts (more of him later) and myself. Paddy Patterson, a nice chap, was with our crowd at Chigwell (pre-second front) and enjoyed a beer or two with us in the "Bald Faced Stag" at Buckhurst Hill. My memory of Phil Scholfield was of him and his permanent companion, whose name I regret I can not remember, going off to dispersal to do their DIs and playing an interminable game of portable chess. Phil also had a lovely bass singing voice and was a member, along with myself and others, in the Padre's hymn-singing group. We had declined to form a service and sermons congregation but agreed to meet once a week to sing hymns. "Guide Me O Lord" was a great favourite.

I too remember a Cpl McQuade (didn't he have a flat in Valletta?) and also the unfortunate Ginger Clarke. Lots of us had surnames beginning with "F" or "M" and perhaps "P". I recall escapes by Freddy Pitts and a chap called, appropriately, Dusty Miller. Freddy was the sole occupant of a billet which got a direct hit. He had been sheltering under a Macdonald type bed covered with bed biscuits near the door. The door fell across his bed and protected him from falling masonry. He emerged looking very much like a "dusty miller".

Miller had himself had taken shelter in a hole in the wall of a quarry near the Siggiewigi dispersal area when a bomb fell into the quarry. He too emerged looking like his namesake.

I remember Sam Halstead, Joe Cook, Arnold Lister, Fred Green and Frank Clarke. I don't remember Sgt Mollison but I do remember Flight Sergeant Jock Forest of 46 Squadron, Beauforts. I wonder if he did "get his mention".

Who will recall Feathers-Davies, whose Flying officers impression made him stand out. I recall him having a small sandbag emplacement on top of "G" Shelter where, armed with a "K" gun, he opened up on kites approaching the main runway.

"How did F-D, get on in the last raid?"

"Oh! Two ME's and probably a Spit!"

I also remember him despatching a stray dog after some misguided MP had only lamed it.

During one spell a transit aircrew who had lost their kits either commandeered or pranged shared a billet with us airmen. One crew consisted of Jimmy Jordon (a navigator I think) who when flying wore, at his mother's insistence, red flannel long combinations. He was a fanatical player at craps and loved to drag non-gamblers like myself into the game. The pilot was a tubby Englishman who was ragged unmercifully by his fellow aircrew, which included a Tasmanian who spent all his spare time in front of a mirror saying "Jeez, I'm a handsome bastard!" Also there was a Welshman and a French Canadian. All their aircrew pay was spent on pay day. They sponged on us gullible airmen for the rest of the fortnight.

Who remembers W/O Stone, who was sent from Uxbridge to instil some discipline into the already seasoned ground staff? It wasn't long before he became one of the lads. I have a snap of him on stage at the concert in the Poor House. Also on the snap was Harold Holt, who was a genius at organising stage shows.

As a result of enemy action we were forced to bed down wherever we could, and as a result we were constantly changing billets and companions. One such billet contained such pleasant inmates as Corporal Papworth, Ginger Johnson, Jock Gordon, Ted Kitchen, Andy Linton and Monty Greenberg. Papworth was a memorable character who, among other things, taught me how to play Bridge. I most remember him for going airborne as a passenger in a Spit. We were having trouble with radios going off-tune when flying at altitude and he crouched behind the pilot in an effort to calculate the degree of returning a set when airborne. This problem eventually disappeared when we were later supplied with radios with quartz crystals. Ginger Johnson I liked very much. His home town was Preston near to where I live and whenever I visit the town I look out for him; so far no luck.

In another billet two of my companions were Stew Harris and Milt Hurd, both of whom were surviving victims of the Polio outbreak. Milt was a Canadian by birth and was heard of in Blighty post-war. Stew Harris lived in Southport for a while and visited my home for a chat and a drink.

Yet another billet, the "Song and Dance" hut, was blessed with a piano and a number of airmen who played or attempted to play guitars and mandolins. Among those present were Merrie England, Dutch Holland, Ireland and France (myself). Again Fred Foster played the piano, varying between Chopin and Fats Waller, his two favourite musicians.

One other billet contained two Yorkshiremen: Steve Ball and Wally Miles. Steve had been a butcher in Civvy Street and, while our thoughts were always centred on food, he claimed he could have one of the numerous goats ready for the oven in ten minutes. Wally suffered badly from bad feet, which prevented him from walking to dispersal very often.

Eventually we ran out of billets and were transferred to Tax-Biex to a lovely villa. Fellows I remember there were Sandy Sandbach and Jessie James (whose claim to fame was based on his sister being a member of the then famous Dagenham Girl Pipers). Included in my snaps from there were Knocker Knox and the famous George "Carter Patterson" Meadows.

Memories of Luqa are not all enemy action. In one incident whilst working on a kite I heard the shout: "Tea wagon up!". With a fellow airman I dashed towards the queue and in our haste we knocked down a couple of squaddies. To my utter delight they turned out to be lads from my home village who, along with other Lancashire Fusiliers, were helping to refuel and rearm our aircraft.

Another incident which will be remembered by many on Luqa concerned a shot-up Maryland trying to land on the main runway without brakes. To overshoot would mean crashing into the quarry. It was a boiling hot day and the heated air rising from the runway was frustrating every attempt by the pilot to get her down as near as possible to the start of the runway. Eventually, after many unsuccessful attempts, he managed to touch down and came hurtling down the runway, at the bottom of which he revved his engines and slewed around without capsizing the plane. By this time a large crowd had assembled and the gallant pilot was greeted with a roar of cheers as he climbed out with his airmen … whose shirts, I remember, were black with sweat.

I also recall at the time that "Warby" (Adrian Warburton DSO and Bar, DFC and Two Bars, DFC (USA)) was reported missing. We were resting with closed eyes outside the section – Bill Mills, "Lucy" Atwell and a few others – when Bill opened one eye and said, "Wasn't that Warby going into the section?" And so, yet again, it was.

Another memorable character was the RAF officer, Powell-Sheddon. For a time he was controller at Luqa and threatened, with a gun, anyone who failed to take proper cover during an air raid.

Finally, my last lot of names, comes from the Orderly Room List prepared by the aforementioned Reg Frost and Bill Vernon.

"Slim" Ayres from fly in Cambridgeshire, Bill Burrows from a pub in Hounslow, Wally Cook from Wimbledon, Jock Crawford from Norwich, Jack Golding from Lincoln, "Len" Harvey from Leeds, Frank Kaye from Barnsley, "Pete" Knight from Surrey, Reg Noakes from Nottingham, "Dai" Morgan from Cardiff, "Mac" McCormack, guitarist from Huyton, Liverpool, "Pem" Pemberton from Lytham, Bert Prior from Dagenham, "Paddy" Roy from County Cork, Bernis Smith from Leeds, "Mick" Sullivan from Holborn, "Vergie" Virgo from Trowbridge, Sid Waters, our 'intelligence' man from Salisbury, "Bill" Whittle from Cardiff, Eric Withnell from Blackpool and Ernie Yallop from Cambridge.

If any of the above mentioned are still alive "good luck to you!"

5. THE LIFE & DEATH OF MV *DEUCALION*

Interview with Captain Ramsay Brown - Master of the MV Deucalion

We were bound for Malta with a cargo of tons of military stores. I gave orders to the gunners before we reached the danger zone not to wait for my orders but to fire at any plane which came within 1,000 yards but to be sure that the aircraft was well within range before opening fire.

During the evening of 11th August 1942 there was an air attack at dusk. All the guns of the convoy opened fire, putting up a terrific barrage which drove off the enemy aircraft without damage to any of our ships. On the 12th at about 0900 there was a high-level attack by Heinkels, dropping their bombs from 3-4,000 feet. We hit and brought down one of these planes with our after gun. The Major, a Royal Artillery officer and passenger, was at this gun, and he, together with all the other gun crew and the Second Officer, saw five or six direct hits on the Heinkel, causing it to turn over and over before it crashed into the sea off our port quarter. I do not think any other ship was firing at this particular plane and I am quite sure that it was our fire which brought it down. We damaged another plane, which flew away with black smoke pouring from it, but it was not seen to crash. Again no damage was done to any ships of the convoy.

I knew there were submarines about at this time and was keeping a strict look-out for them. During the afternoon I sighted the periscopes of two submarines close to our starboard bow and ahead of the convoy. As one periscope was about 20 degrees off my starboard bow I ordered the man on the starboard bridge to fire at it in order to attract the attention of an HMS vessel which was directly off us. I also signalled to her, stating that I had sighted two periscopes, but they replied that they did not think it was a submarine, merely the bow wave from one of the destroyers. I swung over the helm in order to ram, but the submarine dived, almost under my prow. I signaled again, this time to a destroyer of the "Hunt" Class on my port beam; she at once made contact and dropped eight depth charges. A little later we saw a huge patch of oil on the water. I think she destroyed the submarine.

At 13.20 local time another heavy high-level air attack developed, conducted by a large number of Heinkel 111s, five of which seemed to concentrate on my ship. We were still in our correct position in the convoy and were steaming at 13½ knots, steering approximately east. Weather was fine with good visibility, with a smooth sea and light airs. All the armament we could bring to bear was fired, but we sustained three near misses off the starboard side, two off the port side and one direct hit. Of the three on the starboard side, one fell close off the starboard bow, one abreast of No.2 hatch and the third amidships, which went through the boat which was swung out. The two on the port side fell abreast of Nos 1 and 2 holds; all five bombs exploded within 10-15 feet of the hull. The direct hit was caused by a bomb which went through No.6 derrick on the starboard side, penetrated the main deck into No.5 hold and came out through the ship's side below the waterline and then exploded. The planes attacked from fine on the port bow, flying together in no particular formation; all six bombs were dropped from a height of 4,500 feet.

Whilst this examination was going on, some greasers took it upon themselves to lower Nos 6 and 7 lifeboats and pull away from the ship. Shortly afterwards a destroyer appeared on the scene and I ordered these men to return to the ship at once, as I had decided to carry on. They refused at first but eventually came back and climbed on board. The boats were hoisted. The Chief Engineer reported all well in the engine room, and although we were perceptibly lower in the water, our freeboard being only 3ft 6in as against the former 6ft 3in, I decided we could proceed with comparative safety. I passed this information and my decision to the destroyer, who from then acted as guide, as we had lost an hour through the greasers leaving the ship and had fallen well astern of the convoy. Later it was found that the compass had been badly affected by the bombing and I took steps to remedy this. In the evening it was found that compass errors were creeping back to normal.

At about 1430 we got under way again. The Chief Officer and I examined the damage in No.5 hold and he went down the escape hatch to the tunnels, which smelt strongly of petrol. On his return he reported that tunnels and shaftings were intact, with no sign of leakage. From slow speed I now increased to full, about 16¼ knots, but after a period it was found that oil from No.1 tank was pumping itself out of the vents and water started to appear in No.2 hold through No.l well. Three pumps were put in this compartment and on our reducing speed to 12½ knots it was found that we were gaining on the water, and we finally dried the hold.

The destroyer signaled to enquire if we could increase speed and rejoin the convoy, but I said the strain on the ship at 16¼ knots was too much and we were doing our maximum safe speed at 12 knots. She told us to keep as close as possible to the African Coast. We did so, and were getting on nicely with every hope of getting to Malta when we were spotted by an enemy reconnaissance plane at about 17.00.

At 19.46 two planes attacked. I put the helm hard over as three bombs were dropped, two exploding thirty feet astern and one off the port bow 20 feet away. There was no apparent damage from these bombs and we continued.

At 21.20 on 12th August, just after sunset when the light was very bad, two planes attacked simultaneously, the first from the port quarter and the second from the starboard bow. Both planes dived steeply with their engines off and the first I knew of the attack, as did the destroyer, was when our gunners opened fire. The first plane flew along the port side without attacking and then flew off, whilst the second flew along the starboard side at a distance of only 50 or 60 feet and dropped a torpedo from a height of about 75 feet.

The torpedo struck the vessel in No.3 hold on the starboard side. There was no sound from the aircraft's engines until after he had dropped his torpedo and the whole attack was so quickly carried out that the planes were on us and away in a flash. The gunners reckoned they hit the starboard plane but it was not seen to crash. The destroyer saw the torpedo leave the planes, our guns having drawn their attention to the attack. The Chief Officer thought two torpedoes were dropped.

The torpedo struck below the waterline in No.3/5 hold on the starboard side, the starboard tail shaft snapped and immediately the octane spirit ignited, flames rising twice the height of the mast. In a few minutes the stern part of the ship was a blazing inferno and I realised the ship was doomed, so I gave the order to abandon ship.

The men on the poop could not get past the flames but two or three of them walked along the outside of the rail and reached the forward end of the ship. One boat had been destroyed by the direct hit we had received earlier in the day, but we got the other five boats away successfully. No.2 boat went with a run, owing to the forward fall jamming and having to be cut, which upended the boat, spilling the men and my ship's papers into the water. Some of the men managed to get the boat waterborne and climbed into her.

I told the Chief Officer to get all available rafts overboard, as I knew the gun crews aft and anyone else in or on the poop could not possibly get to their boat stations because of the wall of flame. The Chief Officer, Mr Ogilvie, personally took the matter in hand and was of great assistance to me then and throughout the whole passage, showing zeal, coolness and ability of the first order.

Somebody on the after deck managed to release the after rafts. One raft on the poop was blown into the air by the blast and came down on top of a Seaman gunner on the poop. The men were at their guns. Two of my Midshipmen, J.S Gregson and P.P. Bracewell dragged the raft off, got the man out and found that he had a broken thigh, a broken arm, lacerations to the other arm and facial injuries. These two boys dragged him to the ship's side and threw him overboard, then Gregson dived in after him and swam with him to the destroyer, a really gallant and plucky action for a boy of only 18.

We were not long in getting into the boats, the Chief Officer and I being the last to leave at about 2125, the after deck by this time being awash, the ship burning furiously and the ammunition in the square of No.6 hatch exploding at intervals. We pulled round, picking up men from the water and off the rafts and then rowed over to the destroyer.

I reported to the captain and asked him to put a shell into the engine room of my ship to sink her. She was burning furiously and the ammunition on top of the petrol tanks was beginning to explode. I knew we had TNT in the next hold. The destroyer steamed round the vessel and threw a depth charge, which landed on the deck but did not explode.

We were all on board the destroyer by 22.00 and by this time she was silhouetted against the flames from our vessel. We knew the U-boats were in the vicinity, so making a final circle of my vessel the destroyer left the scene about 22.30, the after deck being awash and flames creeping forward towards the after end of the superstructure. I knew the ship could not last long, but did not see her sink.

The destroyer rejoined the convoy and we remained on her for three days until we reached Malta. In my opinion this was the worst part of the passage, as we were crowded below decks and subjected to constant air attacks; the noise of the guns above our heads and the explosions of the bombs were terrific.

While on board the destroyer we saw the tanker *Ohio* bombed and taken in tow by destroyers. There was no one on board the *Ohio* during part of the time and the captain of the destroyer asked me to collect volunteers from my crew and from amongst the other survivors to man the guns on the *Ohio*. A number of men volunteered and I arranged reliefs for meals for the men who stayed on the damaged vessel throughout one day and night. One of *Ohio*'s guns was out of order but the gunners quickly dismantled this and got it working again. I was having a look round the *Ohio* during the night when I met a man on the after deck who asked me who I was. I told him and then asked who he was. He replied, "I am the captain of this ship," so I returned to the destroyer, leaving the *Ohio* in the hands of her own captain.

We finally arrived at Malta on the 15th August. The gun crews, both naval and army gunners, were all excellent and I never hope to be with a finer body of men. They showed a fine example of coolness and courage, only leaving their posts when ordered to do so, and fought their guns throughout the attacks in an exemplary manner. The after gun's crew brought down at least one Heinkel for certain and damaged others.

I would also like to commend Midshipman J.S. Gregson for his gallantry in saving the life of the gunner, as I have recorded.

After the "Pedestal" convoy the following major awards were given:

- ♦ DSCs to Capt Ramsay Brown and Chief Engineer John Campbell;
- ♦ DSMs to N.W. Owen (Carpenter), W. McCaughhey (Boatswain) and W. Lawley (Able Seaman)
- ♦ Albert Medal to John S. Gregson, Apprentice.

6.   TA-KALI AIRFIELD

John Alton – RAF

Before Italy entered the war, Ta-Kali was used as a staging post for Ala-Littoria, the Italian National Civil Airline. When I arrived at Ta-Kali in November 1940 the airline building, a small single-storey hut, was in use as Station Headquarters, housing the Station Commander (Group Captain O'Sullivan), his adjutant and the orderly room. The airfield, viewed from the perimeter resembled a huge car park with old vehicles of every description parked there to obstruct any attempt of an airborne landing by the Italians. One clear strip was left for the Hurricane fighters to take off and land.

Senior NCOs were accommodated in the elegant chateau on the edge of the airfield whilst other ranks lived in a disused pottery nearby. This building had a tall factory chimney, two floors and the normal Maltese flat roof – a good vantage point to observe Luqa aerodrome being bombed. The top floor was given to sleeping accommodation with wooden two-tier bunks instead of beds. These were crawling with bed bugs, which had been vigorously attacked with a blow lamp, as evidenced by many charred areas. The ground floor contained the NAAFI, which in early days had sold Farsons Blue (beer), cigarettes and little more. It did contain a piano, however, which accompanied many a sing-song. Also on the ground floor was the dining area and cookhouse. The latter produced tinned "Bully" in many guises, plus the dreadful butter and tinned bacon (although this was something we would have been grateful for 18 months later). Ablutions were primitive and in winter freezing cold. A meagre supply of hot water was generated by a Heath Robinson device which was little more than a steel plate onto which a supply of oil was dripped; once the plate was hot enough, combustion was self-sustaining.

The only other building was probably once a gate hut and was used by the service policemen. Just outside this hut was a flagpole from which the RAF ensign was normally flown. It was the task of the corporal policeman to hoist this ensign at exactly eight o'clock each morning. On one famous occasion this policeman was a few minutes late and was reminded by a stentorian bellow from the Station Commander.

"Corporal Shannon! Have you surrendered the station?"

Regardless of the weather there was no covered shelter in which aircraft could be serviced, so to remedy this a building was erected at the very edge of the airfield and for good measure construction of a dining hall and living accommodation went ahead at the same time, all within a few hundred yards of the airfield. No doubt the enemy was amused by this activity, for as soon as these buildings were completed and occupied they promptly flattened them all, including the new hangar.

Towards the end of 1940 the parked vehicles were removed except for one "open tourer" Austin Seven, which became transport for the newly-arrived Technical Officer. One day, having completed his daily visit to the readiness dispersal area, he started the engine and put it into gear … but nothing happened, the reason being that a couple of pilots had crept up behind and lifted the rear wheels clear of the ground.

The few refuelling vehicles were soon damaged or burnt out, so a lo-cally-developed refueller was introduced. This was an old double-decker bus with a series of fifty-gallon steel drums suitably interconnected and mounted on the upper deck to allow fuel to pass under gravity to the aircraft. The experiment was short-lived and must have been a nightmare for the drivers.

After the removal of the parked vehicles 'anti-airborne landing' mines were placed in groups around the perimeter of the airfield. Following a suitable airborne landing warning similar items would also have been placed at strategic points on the airfield. Once in position a vertical an-tenna was fitted and deflection of this would set the mine off. It was the duty of the squadron armourers to service these mines and one day whilst this operation was being carried out there was a loud detonation, followed by a cloud of dust. The armourer concerned had simply vanished and had to be posted "missing", even though it was obvious what had happened.

Church parades were held regularly with the Padre arriving from HQ Valletta and driving to where the pilots and ground crews were standing-by ready for an alert, where he commenced the act of worship. One airman was not involved; it was his duty to man the telephone. Sometimes the telephone would ring during the service, closely followed by the airman shouting: "SCRAMBLE! SCRAMBLE!" Hymn books would go flying as ground crews and pilots rushed to their aircraft, engines were started and away went the Hurricanes in a great cloud of dust. The Padre would then quietly collect his hymn books, climb into his vehicle and depart for Valletta. I often wondered what his thoughts were.

Before the formation of the Malta Night Fighter Unit, one Hurricane and pilot remained at readiness at Ta-Kali and at dusk it was the duty of the ground crew to bolt two plates above the exhaust stubs, to prevent the pilot's vision being affected by the exhaust flames. There was no flare path at Ta-Kali, which made this operation hazardous. I can not recall any of the night fighters shooting down an enemy aircraft at this time.

Winter in Malta was never very pleasant and this was especially so at Ta-Kali. When the weather at night became particularly inclement the Medical Officer used to authorise a "rum ration" for any ground crew on duty. After a period of rain the airfield would turn into a morass and the Hurricanes would have to be manoeuvred to the start of the runway from which they took off for Luqa, from where they operated until Ta-Kali dried out. This was never popular with the ground crews, for it meant a very early start and a cold bus ride to Luqa and on return each day the billet was cold, as there was no heating, and furthermore there were no facilities for drying wet clothing. The warmest place was in bed, provided that an air raid did not materialise, for then it was obligatory to leave one's 'pit' and take cover.

During the latter part of 1940 and through 1942, in common with the rest of the island, Ta-Kali had its share of enemy activity, sometimes strafing by Macchi 202s or ME109s; the latter often practiced dive bombing and for some reason a crackle of cannon fire signalled the release of a bomb. Mostly these raids were unpleasant, but occasionally they had a humorous side, for example I remember one morning in early 1942 the ground crew was using an old bus as a shelter whilst awaiting a fighter scramble. One airman, on entering the bus, remarked that a couple of Hampdens (RAF twin-engine bombers) were coming in from St Paul's Bay. Within seconds the roar of aircraft coupled with cannon fire demonstrated that the 'Hampdens' were in fact ME109s. They departed as quickly as they had arrived, leaving one Hurricane to completely burn out. The ground crew was about ten yards from it. Just a slight deflection of aim by the Luftwaffe pilot would have wiped out half the ground crew at Ta-Kali.

Ta- Kali's worst period of travail was surely on the 20th and 21st March 1942, as this followed the arrival of the first Spitfires. On the evening of the 20th March every available Luftwaffe bomber crew in Sicily took off, formatted and headed for Malta. This armada of JU88s and ME109s concentrated on Ta-Kali and dropped more than 100 tons of bombs on and around the airfield. The raid was obviously aimed at the Spitfires and Hurricanes. The Luftwaffe believed that the partially-excavated site on the Imtarfa side of the aerodrome was an underground hangar and a number of JU88s dropped special armour-piercing bombs capable of penetrating rock to a depth of 15 metres. In fact, the task of excavating that particular area had been abandoned because the rock had proved unsuitable.

The following morning the Luftwaffe returned again and this time the armada numbered 106 JU88s and about 100 ME109s as cover. They released 180 tons of bombs on Ta-Kali and German records state that this was the first attempt at carpet bombing by the Luftwaffe. The writer sat this one out in a slit trench on the edge of the airfield and probably prayed harder than ever before or since.

Four caves had successfully been excavated around the perimeter of the airfield to house the administrative offices, the armoury and the fuel dump. The latter contained precious aircraft fuel in 4-gallon tins. Apparently a member of the stores staff entered this cave with a hurricane lamp alight and the contents were completely lost. It was rumoured that the Station Commander had to be forcibly restrained from summarily shooting the offender.

Following the two heavy raids the airfield looked like a lunar landscape and the Luftwaffe pilots reported that it was completely destroyed. But the Army (who never received the accolade they richly deserved) immediately got to work and had the craters filled in time to receive a further supply of Spitfires, which were already on the way. On arrival they met a welcoming committee of 70 JU88s, complete with fighter escort.

In this raid a lot of bombs fell on the surrounding villages. A particularly large bomb fell outside a hotel in Rabat which housed RAF officers from Ta-Kali; six were killed outright and the seventh, an American pilot, died in hospital. It was noted that on this raid some large bombs were fastened together by stout chains.

My memories of Ta-Kali for the following several months are confused; of just one long, continuous raid, which indeed it almost was. All the old landmarks had gone and following a near miss the old pottery had been demolished by explosives. The airfield was a mass of filled-in bomb craters and the remains of downed aircraft, both German and British, lay around the perimeter. Food rationing was at its most severe and one felt continually hungry. Cigarettes could sometimes be obtained at Black Market prices (in packets marked "NAAFI Stores for HM Forces"). Footwear was very difficult to acquire and I recall I was delighted to accept a pair of army ankle boots when my own shoes fell apart.

I was fortunate to be promoted to Senior NCO rank and posted away from the island in August 1942. I boarded a DC3 aircraft at Luqa and landed in Egypt the following morning, just in time for the breakfast I had dreamed of for months – but alas it proved far too much for a stomach grown used to meagre rations of "Bully" and hard-tack biscuits.

I think that for everyone who was there during the war, memories of Malta are very personal; different people remembering different things. I know of one case where, after a lapse of nearly fifty years, a former groundcrew member had a serious nervous breakdown, which was clinically attributed to his time on Malta. Perhaps my own bad memories are still present, but (happily) suppressed.

7.   TWO SHIPWRECKS AND A SIEGE

R.J.P. Claxton – Royal Navy, New Zealand

I suppose my war began on 17th September 1940, the night our ship, HMS *Kent*, was torpedoed off Bordia, 'Fort Capuzzo'. We were scheduled to bombard Bordia at midnight, accompanied by two 'tribal' class destroyers: *Mohawk* and *Nubian*. We were already to commence our bombardment of over 1,000 Italian troops under canvas when suddenly a star shell lit the sky and then THUMP! they got us on the port side aft in our screws. Thirty-three hands were lost, including our Commander, Hall.

Quite a battle erupted whilst we drifted, but HMS *Nubian* got us under tow and the most beautiful sight I have ever seen was the Eastern Mediterranean Fleet at sunrise in the morning – battleships, cruisers, aircraft carriers and destroyers, helping to ward off aerial attacks by the Italians. Mind you, at 30,000 feet it was not difficult!

On entering Alexandria harbour the lads on all ships turned out to give us three rip-roaring 'hip hoorays' with voices, caps and hats.

After a rushed patch-up job in the floating dock in Alexandria Harbour and also being rammed by one of our own submarines coming in to tie up alongside, we were eventually off and through Suez, round the Cape and up to Freetown to join a massive convoy and proceed to the UK – all this after being away on the China Station from June 1938 to December 1940.

Then home on 21 days leave before returning to Eastney Gunnery School in Pompey for an AA III Gunnery Course and a draft chit known as an MW1. Then, amidst lots of secrecy, I boarded a train in Chatham Dockyard at the end of April 41, having no idea what was on or where we were going, but noticed it was getting cooler as the night wore on.

We arrived at Gourock in Scotland, where there were lots of AA Ratings and Signal men; I was just a young Able Seaman. They had different numbers: MV-II, MV-III, MV-IV and so on. We loaded our bags and hammocks onto a tender and off we went to find out that MV stood for Merchant Vessel. Mine was a ship on its maiden voyage called the *Empire Song*, which along with *Clan Campbell, Clan Chattan, Clan Lament* and *New Zealand Star* were on tank convoy 'Tiger'.

When I got up the rope ladder that was the last we saw of the other lads. There were six ratings to each ship plus two signal men. As soon as we were aboard the convoy sailed, destination once again, 'unknown'. Luckily for me a lieutenant who had served on HMS *Kent* was the Naval Officer attached to *Empire Song*. We were escorted by units of the Western Approaches, consisting of two destroyers. The Naval Officer had been a pilot of our Walrus aircraft on HMS *Kent*. I cannot remember his name but he suggested we 'splice the mainbrace'. Next day when the tots of rum were served I was so pleased to learn that whoever was responsible for the catering had not forgotten the 'bubbly' which a little later on we were to indulge in.

The convoy headed south and I got friendly with the Chief Engineer, a fine Scotsman who told me we were bound for Suez – which meant Port Suez and running the gauntlet through the Mediterranean. Having only left it four months earlier I knew that by this time Jerry and his Stukas were in Italy and Sicily in large numbers.

We wrote our last letters on 6th May 41 because our escorting destroyers were being relieved by the Fleet from Gibraltar and returning to Portland. We sailed through the Straits of Gibraltar on 7th May under darkness and next morning it was like it had been on 17th September 1940 on HMS *Kent*. The sea was one mass of ships, battleships, cruisers, destroyers and at least two aircraft carriers. I believe Admiral Somerville was the Admiral in charge on one of the battleships.

The sea was blue, the rum a nice maroon colour and the ships all going nicely at 14 knots when suddenly an enemy reconnaissance plane spotted the convoy just 12 hours out of Gibraltar...

Two hours later all hell broke loose. I had never seen anything like it. There were Junkers 88s, Heinkels, bomb splashes, small AA, large AA, pom-poms – you name it. It was horrendous. We had several very near misses with aircraft from our carriers helping to drive off the Jerries, but during the day we lost one destroyer.

On the *Empire Song* we had two single Bofors guns for us to man and there were some DEM lads with a larger gun on the stern. Jerry resumed his attack at about 4pm but came off second best as they lost many aircraft which were shot down by our carriers' planes.

We ploughed on towards Suez. I had just been relieved on the Bofors at midnight when THUMP something hit the ship or vice-versa. It was a repetition of my experience on HMS *Kent*. The ship still made way and then THUMP – another one! Now we had really come to a stop and I could see that a lot of smoke and steam was drifting aft along the whole length of the ship and there was a weird smell.

"What's happening?" I asked the Chief Engineer, who was turning a valve.

"We hit two mines and the Old Man is abandoning ship," he replied.

My Abandon Ship position was No.2. Boat, with a signalman whose name I recall was Whitfield. We had a mixed crew aboard of Somalis, Indians, Chinese, Scotch and English. The Somalis and Indians panicked and were lowering boats stern first, bow first and sometimes 'bang' into the water. After almost being submerged in our boat, as there were too many aboard, we managed to let go the falls and hare off towards the destroyer HMS *Foresight*. As we were making no way I decided to go over the side and swim for it; luckily the *Foresight* remained stationary and occasionally put on her searchlights briefly. I clambered up the safety nets until some welcome matelot pulled me in, along with some other lucky ones who had made it. I had just put my feet aboard when there was an almighty explosion; the *Empire Song* had blown up and disappeared below the waves. There were cries of help of all sorts coming from out of the dark sea. How many were saved I do not know, but we were given some rum, a sandwich and a good old 'cuppa'. The *Foresight* left the convoy and headed for Malta to drop us survivors off. I believe that two merchant ships were sunk, but I have read a book which stated that the *New Zealand Star* was damaged by mines but did not sink. HMS *Foresight* was attacked on her way to Malta but we arrived safely and all of the survivors were despatched to Imtarfa Hospital with fuel poisoning and, of course, shock after seeing a merchant ship blow up on a dark night and tanks flying through the air (she was loaded with a large cargo of ammunition and tanks). I remember one lad going mad on the *Foresight* because he had received a shrapnel wound to his skull. He went after one of the officers, apparently in the belief that *Foresight* was always where the trouble was.

Whilst recuperating in Imtarfa Hospital I saw an army lieutenant walk by who had 2nd Devons on his shoulder straps. I called out to him and asked him if he knew anyone by the name of Harold Flood. He replied "Yes" he was a sergeant in the Devon's band and played the French horn. I had not seen my brother for over seven years, when I was just a kid. I was not even sure if that was the name of his Regiment, but in a short time my brother was at my bedside and as soon as I was able, about 10 days later, we were swimming together in St Paul's Bay.

After being released from hospital I was sent to Lazeretto submarine base, where I spent some time as QM on shift-work at the base, and it was here that I had my own private chat with Lord Louis Mountbatten, then captain of HMS *Kelly*, which was lying out in the stream with HMS *Kipling*, HMS *Kashmere* and other ships. I felt very honoured until bombs started falling perilously close and Lord Louis advised me to take cover under the granite of Lazeretto Base. All he wanted to do was to get out to HMS *Kelly*. I left him there after he had asked me how I managed to be in Malta, shore-based.

I was transferred to Hal Far aerodrome after about 6 weeks and at-tached to the Fleet Air Arm's 830 Squadron, which soon was joined by 828 squadron. I was at Hal Far from August 1941 to August 1943, where I became known as 'the rebel'. The base was under the command of the RAF fighter squadrons of Hurricanes and later Spitfires. The main fighter base was Ta Kali. Being a matelot I liked my tot, but we were not allowed it as it was a RAF establishment. This annoyed me and I tried to get away from the base to get to sea, but I was denied, so at Xmas 1941, after obtaining a large White Ensign from Lazeretto Base, I hauled down the RAF Flag, attached the White Ensign to the halyards, attached the RAF flag underneath and duly hoisted both flags up the to the top. I was sent for by the Duty RAF Officer and made to haul down the offending flag and re-hoist the RAF Flag and was placed under escort for the remainder of Xmas.

I had always had a thing about being in the Navy but this had nothing to do with the RAF. I was given a caution and sent to join HMS *Jade*, a minesweeper, but whilst I was ashore the *Jade* was sunk, so I had to return to Hal Far once again!

My brother's regiment was stationed at Tarxein, about 4½ miles away, and his band regularly played at the RAF Barracks.

830 and 828 Squadrons had Swordfish and Albacore aircraft under which we had to place torpedoes and mines, ready for night operations. Nearly every night the planes went off, either to attack an enemy convoy or a harbour in Sicily. The air gunners, who were billeted with us, often came back with wondrous tales of a plane they had been in or of their torpedoes striking home on their targets.

I also had the task of cleaning the mess room toilets and did my turn on the fire tender to push the aircraft about, as petrol was very scarce. We had to fill in bomb holes on the runways. At times when we were out there with the old Bedford truck filling in the holes Jerry would fly in and strafe us in Messerschmitts, so we made for the caves not far from Hal Far. During the Siege we had our .303 rifles with us and ammunition and as Jerry flew parallel to the cliffs with their speed about 300-350 miles per hour we used to aim and fire at the planes or throw a tin into the sea below and see who could hit it. We were able to pick up lots of .303 ammo from the Spitfire and Swordfish aircraft, as their ammo had to be changed if not used after a certain amount of time.

I well recall one tragic incident. Sometimes I used to go to a shelter which was not underground but had a very thick concrete roof with steel rafters and was bricked round on all sides. On this particular day we received information that 100 plus aircraft were heading for Hal Far, so I decided not to use my normal shelter but instead ran the extra distance to another 30ft deep shelter. The concrete-roofed shelter received a direct hit and some 60 RAF and Army personnel were killed. Others were trapped under that thick concrete roof but because we had no serviceable crane or bulldozer we could not get these poor souls out. They perished slowly and nothing could be done.

I remember at Xmas I wanted to put some decorations in our billet so I saved all the old Tombola (Bingo) tickets, cut them up into strips and joined them together into colourful paper chains.

Being hungry continuously was the hardest part. I saw men fight for the last bit of potato in a tin of 'meat and veg' and was fired on by a Maltese farmer for pulling up the foliage where his potatoes were planted; the spuds were only the size of marbles. When we went ashore we took a 'bread chit' so that if we found somewhere to eat we might possibly get some bread.

I was involved in unloading HMS *Breconshire* in Kalafrana Bay, where she was bombed and set on fire. As she turned upside-down we got the precious contents out of her hold by going in through the steel plates on the bottom of the ship. They asked for volunteers and my first thought was that perhaps I may be able to get some tobacco, but all we got was a big 'thank you' after we had emptied out the dear old *Breconshire*. Malta owed a lot to the fine ship and crew.

To stand and watch from about six miles away the Stukas bombing the Grand Harbour and the AA Batteries assembled around its perimeter putting up a 'box barrage'. One could actually see the bursting of the shells in the air, which appeared like a square from a distance; as the Stukas dived in they were hit by bursting shells. There would of course have been ships in the Grand harbour.

Despite everything morale was great and somehow we were able to get 'Ambete' red or white. I think the ride on the bus from Valletta to Hal Far was worse than the bombing.

After having a nice night's 'kip' for a shilling in one of the many sleeping outlets we went down the 'Gut' and filled up with a few bottles of blue and Ambete. I remember Josey, who owned the place, had not called me to catch the bus back to Hal Far. I got dressed and went out of the front door, just down from the Lucky Wheel, to find that both ends of the 'Gut' had been bombed. I had to climb over mountains of dirty rubble to get out, amazed that I had slept through it all. One needed a lot of luck to stay alive; the only injury I received was a broken wrist dodging a bomb at Hal Far whilst manning a Lewis Gun on the aerodrome.

I put in my request to return to sea but St Angelo decided I should go home so I departed on a Sunderland from Kalafrana Bay with an Australian flight crew. At Gibraltar I was taken off to allow VIPs to fly home while I continued on HMS *Liverpool*.

I later heard that the Sunderland was shot down in the Bay of Biscay by a Focke-Wulf FW-190. Lucky Old Me!

8.   WHEN NATURE CALLS

H.W. (Nat) Gold – 830 Squadron, Fleet Air Arm

My pilot and I had just completed a very hazardous torpedo attack and were making a return rendezvous when the marker flare suddenly went out. We circled for some time but there were no other friendly navigation lights. Maybe the CO thought we had not made it and had proceeded on his way back to Malta, leaving us to find our own way. Then some loud mutterings came through the Gosport tube from my pilot – familiar four letter words – and all I could do was grunt, he being an Officer and a Gentleman.

I knew in a very short while he would be asking for a course to steer. I was still standing up, peering into the darkness, hoping I could catch a glimpse of some lights, but knew it to be futile. The night was inky black and all that could be seen were millions of stars and blackness; it felt as though we had left the earth and were floating in space. I had to pinch myself to make sure I was still alive.

I sat down and checked the radio. All seemed well, but there were very noisy atmospherics. My Mae West was slightly inflated and I raised the portion behind my head to act as a pillow against the hard additional petrol tank in the Observer's cockpit. I tried to get comfortable and relax for a while, but it wasn't easy. Suddenly I heard my pilot's voice again. '

Ah!' I thought. 'He wants that course to steer' … but no.

"Have you got a tin?" he asked "I want to pee."

"Yes." I replied.

"Pass it to me."

"OK." I replied. A simple request which proved that our old Swordfish had no modern convenience.

Little did I realise what I had let myself in for. ..

I found the float tin, removed the lid and threw it overboard. I carefully removed the contents without pulling the cord so that it would not ignite when it contacted the water. I threw this overboard and observed later that it had ignited. I realised I could not reach my pilot, so I thought of standing on the gun steps, but these were too far back. The only way would be to stand on the seat, so with the tin tightly gripped in my right hand I attempted to stand … but I had forgotten my "G-string" which unceremoniously yanked me back. I fell off the seat and banged my funny bone on the gun ring. Result? Repetitions of my pilot's four-letter words. I grabbed the Gosport and yelled to him that I would have to unhook my G-string and that he should for Christ's sake hold the kite level as I would be passing the tin over the top.

"OK, hurry up" he replied.

I unhooked the G-string and stood on the seat, but couldn't see anything to hang onto. The shape of the tank made gripping an impossibility. I suddenly thought of the vent pipe on top of the tank. I felt around for it in the darkness and located it. Gripping firmly, I started to pull myself forward, but my Mae West and the hooks on my harness were in the way. I wondered if I should hook my parachute on. No, that would be even more hopeless. Once again I tried, lifting my head and chest up slightly, whereupon the slipstream distorted my cheek and mouth to one side. I felt like a "God-damn-Gangster" saying "Listen yooos guys…"

I attempted a chuckle. Then my helmet and goggles started to slew round and I had to get back again. After straightening the offending articles I tightened the straps as tight as I could. Once again I proceeded and was now becoming experienced. I found the vent pipe first time. I pulled and then panicked; supposing this vent snapped off or suppose we dropped into an air pocket? My legs went like jelly. I tried to dismiss these thoughts. Impossible. I pulled hard with my knuckles, gripping the vent with one hand and the tin with the other. I tried speeding things up and raised my arm in a Nazi salute, muttering "Heil Hitler" and lay across the tank giggling.

I felt so stupid and helpless to be in this predicament several thousand feet above the Mediterranean. I managed to get my arm down and quickly thought out my next move. The only way to beat the slipstream would be to sneak the tin up along the surface of the tank. This worked. I pushed the tin forward and came into contact with something solid but soft. I lifted my arm slightly and brought the tin down and to my great joy I felt it being pulled. I let go and quickly slithered back. Once my feet were firmly planted on the cockpit floor I hurriedly re-hooked my "G-string". At last I felt safe, so I grabbed the Gosport and yelled to my pilot, "Have you got it O.K.?"

"Yes" he replied, "but you took your time."

"I will explain why later!" I yelled.

During the next few moments the Old Swordfish made some very erratic movements and after several more minutes, I once again heard my pilot's voice. "Stand by for throwing overboard!"

I ducked down and got close into the side of the cockpit until I heard him declare "Tin overboard!"

I sat up, my legs still like jelly. I had been more nervous than during the torpedo attack.

"Never again," I muttered. "Next time Sir can pee in his trousers!"

9.   AIR RAID

Junior

Over the harbour they came in their flights,
Carrying the Swastika. Oh! what a sight.
The Spits and the Hurries roared up to meet,
To harry and punish and then to defeat.

The Gunners are busy, the sky is all black,
The smoke and the fire is all from the flak,
The bombs bring down houses, churches and all,
And the petrol explodes in a great fireball.

The hangers are ruined, the craft on the ground
Receive the same treatment, an almighty pound.
The fire bell rings as we rush out to slave,
At what can be rescued any bodies to save.

A pilot is trapped in his burning plane,
We rush to his aid, we can feel his pain,
No effort is spared but the task is beyond,
The efforts of those who wish to respond.

Suddenly its silence, the enemy gone,
When will this war end? All of this wrong?
Slowly and sadly we go back to bed,
To say a short prayer for the living and dead.

10. THE MALTA POLICE AT WAR

Assistant Commissioner Edward J. Bonnici-Solar

Throughout the war years I covered all five Police Districts in Malta, one or two at a time and for specific purposes. I was in charge of the Water Police when I saw *Ohio* and *Illustrious* limp into the harbour. I duly contacted the captain of the *Ohio* as instructed. With regard to the *Illustrious*, the German planes were not long in coming over to disintegrate her completely. A merchant ship on the other side of dockyard (I think it was the *Essex*) was also badly hit but still floating; a bomb had gone in through the funnel and exploded inside the ship, causing wanton slaughter amongst the crew and stevedores. I had never seen such devastation; my greatest consternation was the moment I skidded on a primary part of human skin.

On another occasion four of us were in a Police motor-boat on our way from Marsa to the Custom House when we savoured an unexpected attack on the harbour. We were soon left alone by the Italian pilot when "forca miseria" he heard the sharp crack of my unprintable blast of Italian, unless he was German, in which case he must have known Italian fluently!

It was late one night when during one of the attacks by German planes I saw from near the Custom House what I reckoned to be a German pilot parachuting down over Senglea. I passed the relative message to Headquarters and then all hell broke loose. It was not a German pilot but a mine, which presumably was meant for the Grand Harbour. Its strong blast reached us, loud and clear, across the harbour.

On another night the Electricity Power Station, which was not far from the Custom House, was hit and a vital bakery at Marsa was set on fire. I jumped into my car and drove straight to Marsa. The fire engine was soon on the spot and water was poured over the roof and the ventilators. Unknown to us a concealed 15,000 volt transformer was at the back of the bakery. Afterwards I wondered why none of us received any shocks, as sparks kept shooting out, eventually making us aware of the danger. An event that followed made me wonder all the more; the following day when it was light I discovered that on my way to Marsa I had driven my car under a very high voltage cable which had come down across the road next to the Power Station. I had missed it by no more than two inches.

One day I went to Sliema to see my family, who I had not seen for about a month. On hearing a drove of German planes on their way inland I rushed out into the street without even bothering to cover my bald head. I then heard a bomb or shell coming down but for some reason could not bring myself to run for cover. I just stood transfixed in the middle of the road. Luckily for me it was not a bomb at all, merely an ack-ack shell cap, which, astonishingly, gave me no more than a light kiss on the tip of my nose.

Another incident concerned a heavy explosion at the mouth of the harbour. As Officer in Charge I got into my police motor boat and was on my way to investigate when suddenly the engine came to a halt and we started to drift towards the shore. It was a blessing in disguise. Italian MT boats were trying to enter the harbour and my brother in the RMA, who was in charge of the guns at that spot, had just received orders to shoot at anything moving in those waters.

Seeing the SS *Talabot* in 1942 fully laden with a dangerous cargo ablaze in the harbour was really heartbreaking. Steps were taken to prevent it exploding and from causing sweeping destruction all round.

Before I move on to experiences in other districts I wish to add a postscript which concerns that rather capricious lady Fate – who could have been more affable than to have me posted to the Water Police! She must have known only too well that although I loved the sea, the sea never loved me. Nowadays when the sea is displayed on television it reminds me that I should have known better than to feel seasick.

When the Opera House in Valletta was bombed and blown up by German planes it so happened that I had just entered Strada Realle (later Kingsway). I only just managed to survive that hair-raising experience.

It was a pitiful sight when I saw an Italian pilot some height over Valletta drifting in the air towards Grand Harbour with a parachute that evidently refused to open. His prayer to the Virgin Mary to help him was loud and clear. He finally crashed into a private garden in Cospicua.

One day whilst in charge of the central part of the island I observed a huge bomb some six feet in length somersaulting on its way down. It landed in a field but there was no explosion. It was made of tin and packed with small incendiary bombs, but luckily did no damage at all.

Over at Hamrun a bomb was released from an enemy plane and was seen at some height on its way from Marsamxett Harbour towards Valletta. It exploded not far from the opera House at the entrance to an air-raid shelter, killing a number of people.

On one particular night a large number of huge delayed-action bombs were dropped all over the island. One of my inspectors accompanied me to try and locate as many as we could in my area. In one of the houses in the High Street at Hamrun a bomb had gone through the roof and ceiling and ended up close to an old woman in a bed. The fallen masonry had killed her. She was carried out and soon afterwards the bomb exploded and demolished the whole building. Further down the same street another bomb had gone through the roof of another house and into the front room. Luckily enough it had gone down an old well. We were in line with this house when the first bomb exploded and it so happened that I ran towards the second house for cover. Luckily, due to the location of the bomb, the house was not completely wrecked. Large building blocks toppled down from the side of the roof, the front door shot out by my side and two young women, who had been inside, crashed straight into me. We did not suffer any serious damage, but tiny pieces of shrapnel had managed to penetrate our uniforms.

On another occasion the central part of the island, particularly Mdina, was inundated with "butterfly bombs" (curious-looking booby-trap devices that would explode if touched); they caused quite a number of casualties. The Bomb Disposal Officer and I visited a garden dotted with a good number of them. Somehow I managed to touch one of them in a narrow passage, but no thanks to Mr Hitler it failed to explode. I may add that the B.D.O. had something to say about this! That very "butterfly bomb" was later dismantled and despatched post-haste to London for the edification of other bomb-disposal men.

Another curious incident I recall was meeting two South African deep-sea divers who were recovering mines from a stricken ship in Marsaxlokk Harbour. They said they had come across two colossal octopuses and refused to go underwater in that area again.

During 1943 and 1944 I was appointed Acting Director of Prisons on five different occasions, whereupon my greatest concern became bomb damage to the prison buildings, especially the main deeps.

11. ESCAPE TO MALTA

H.J. Randall – RAF

The crew of the Beaufort was shot down during a strike on an Axis Convoy in the Mediterranean on Tuesday 28th July 1942 and turned up in Malta the next day. The captain of the Beaufort was Lt E.T. Strevor of Klerksdorp South Africa and the rest of the crew were: Petty Officer W.M. Dunsmore of Mighaull, Liverpool, Sgt J.A. Wilkinson of Auckland, New Zealand, and Sgt A.R. Brown of Timbru, New Zealand. There story is one of the most astonishing of the war and apart from Dunsmore, who had a slight cut on his right arm, they all escaped unscathed.

The story begins with Strevor realising that his aircraft was doomed after releasing his torpedo at a merchant vessel and being badly shot up by flak. When the aircraft hit the sea, Strevor, being in the nose, went under and was quite convinced he was going to drown. However, he clambered clear and joined the rest of the crew in their dinghy. They were only four or five miles from land, but it seemed ten times that distance when they set out to row with their paddles. Their aircraft sank in a minute and a half and after they had been paddling for some time they noticed an Italian float plane circling them. After a few minutes it landed about a hundred yards from them and Strevor swam over to it. He was courteously received and immediately offered a brandy and a cigarette. In a pantomime he explained what had happened, the other three members of the crew were picked up and they too received the same hospitality from their affable captors. The plane then taxied round to point to a harbour in a nearby island.

On getting ashore they were taken to a camp where they met an officer who spoke good English. Their captors suspected that as it was mid-afternoon and the British crew had had nothing to eat since breakfast that they were probably hungry. Our airmen agreed heartily and were taken to the Officers Mess and had set before them a gargantuan repast with an unlimited supply of steak and tomatoes. They also had pressed on them much wine; the Italians explaining that it was much too dangerous a practice to drink water. Cigarettes, incidentally, were offered to them continually and Strevor reckoned that during their short stay he must have received 150. Meanwhile, clothes, even down to their socks, were lent to them by the Italian officers while their own dried in the sun. They were given the run of the mess, the only restriction being that they were politely asked not to run away. Notepaper and envelopes were produced and they were informed that if they cared to write to relations and leave the envelopes unsealed they would be sent off via the Red Cross.

The captives then spent an hour or two playing ping-pong and cards and at about 8pm were offered another meal with the Italian officers which they did not really want, but did not like to refuse, as it might have offended their thoughtful hosts. They consumed large quantities of hors d'oevres followed by liver and vegetables, along with wine, which Dunsmore said they 'drank like water'. They were asked to play bridge but unfortunately none of the four was a bridge player. The Italians said that was pity as they had three very keen players among themselves and had been longing for an Englishman, as they understood that all Englishmen played bridge. A pleasant evening passed and the Italian officers gave up their own rooms when bedtime arrived. The only sense of imprisonment was from the guards posted outside their windows and in the passage outside their door.

In the morning they were woken and given coffee. The Italians apologised for forgetting that Englishmen, unlike Italians, must have a hearty breakfast and asked what they would like. They soon sat down to a breakfast of eggs and more coffee, which was delicious. Their immediate future was uncertain but for the moment there appeared to be no lack of food and Strevor suggested that they should all eat as much as they could while the going was good.

After breakfast photographs were taken outside in the Mess with British and Italians fraternising in gala spirit. One of the Italians expressed the hope that the British would find the internment camp as pleasant and said that they were sorry their captives could not stay longer with them. Our airmen were then taken aboard the Cant float plane again. They had a Corporal as an armed escort and the Cant's crew consisted of the pilot, second pilot, engineer and wireless operator/observer. They took off as, our people thought, for Taranto.

Wilkinson was the only one to see the possibility of capturing the aircraft. He was seated facing the observer, behind whom was the escort with a revolver at his waist. Wilkinson attracted the observer's attention, hit him smack on the jaw, jumped over him and seized the escort's revolver, which he quickly passed to Strevor. They used the corporal's body as a shield when approaching the first pilot, the only other armed Italian, who was seen to be fumbling for his own automatic pistol. Strevor brandished the escort's pistol in true Wild West fashion and held up the co-pilot before he could get at his own weapon. The pilot had meanwhile put the nose down as if to land, but Strevor's pantomime order to pull his stick back – accompanied by the sight of a pistol – made him change his mind. Dunsmore and Brown had meanwhile dealt with the rest of the Italian crew and Strevor took control. The Italians were tied up with rope and their own belts with their hands behind their backs. The tool box was opened and Dunsmore, Wilkinson and Brown armed themselves with vicious-looking wrenches and spanners, the lethal potentialities of which they impressed upon the Italians.

Once the Italian crew saw the game was up they accepted the situation philosophically but looked so unhappy that the British tried to make them more comfortable. The escort corporal was in a bad way, vomiting frequently and Dunsmore, who himself had suffered severely from air sickness, took pity on him, loosened his collar and eventually propped him up against an open window where he felt much better. It was subsequently disclosed that the Corporal had never flown before.

The capture of the aircraft took only a few seconds but Strevor was now faced with the difficulty of having no maps or charts, as the Italians were not carrying them, and not knowing the speed and capacity of the aircraft or how much fuel he would need to make it to Malta. None of the Italians spoke English, but Strevor set the second pilot free and put him on the controls while he made a rough and ready calculation of his own. Strevor had decided to come down in Sicily and trust to luck if he could not make Malta. The Italian steered the courses set by him. Strevor himself took the controls from time to time but there was no danger from the Italian, who had cheerfully summed up the position and indicated that he would do as he was told. At length they saw the 'toe' of Italy below, which enabled Strevor to get some sort of fix and he determined to chance the petrol situation and head for Malta.

As they approached Malta there began what all four of our boys agreed was the most terrifying episode of their trip. They were flying at deck level when three Spitfires attacked them. Brown swung the guns about in an effort to show the fighters that he was not going to fire and Dunsmore took off his vest, which was the only white object that they had on board and trailed it out as a sign of surrender. But still the Spitfires spat and when one of the wings was hit by both machine gun and cannon fire Strevor ordered the pilot to come down on the water. As they did so the engines stopped; they had run out of petrol.

Subsequently they were towed into Malta and Strevor himself personally supervised the comfort and settling in of the Italians in their new home. As he said, it was the least he could do to return the hospitality that he and the others had received. He had it explained to the Italians that he was sorry to have done what he had, but that there was no other course open to him and there was nothing personal in it. The Italians cheerfully agreed with him and the prevailing spirit was most fraternal. One of the

Italians showed his gratitude by opening a bottle of wine from his suitcase, explaining that he was glad to use it so, although it had been destined for other purposes. The Italians had been going on leave as soon s they reached Taranto.

**Lt Strevor, Pilot Officer Dunsmore & Sgt Brown
with the Italian Cant seaplane they captured.**

12.   BOMBS, BOMBS AND MORE BOMBS!

Tich Hill - RAF Luqa and 272 Squadron

It was early September 1941 when I, along with many other airmen, left the Mersey bound for Malta. Of course we did not know where we were going at the time, but we had been issued with warm weather kit at RAF Wilmelow, so anticipated somewhere HOT!

The ship we boarded was a 12,000-ton merchant ship named *Imperial Star* of the Blue Star Line. Immediately after settling in we were paraded and all the armourers were selected to become anti-aircraft gunners and man the ship's Oerlikon guns, so we had a quick course on this, to us, strange weapon. There were four men on each gun with an NCO in charge. I was corporal armourer and had charge of an afterdeck portside gun. Our ship had a bad habit of emitting sparks from its funnel, especially visible at night and we considered this a bad omen.

We sailed west for a day or two, eventually becoming part of a big convoy named "Halberd", consisting of nine ships with 21 escort vessels. One morning one of the seamen told us we had passed Gibraltar during the night, so we were now in the Med. The journey through the Med was pleasant and uneventful until we were into the narrowing waters between Sicily and Algeria… Then all hell broke loose just after mid-day.

We were attacked by a large number of aircraft, several of which were shot down, to the rousing cheers of the watchers on the ships. After the attack the convoy sailed on with no severe damage done, but one seaman who had seen it all before said to us "They'll be back" and sure enough they came back in the evening and things got a bit hotter.

Out of nowhere an Italian bomber screamed over my gun position and seconds later the torpedo struck just below us. The explosion lifted me off the gun and threw me over the hatch cover (lucky that I didn't go the other way). The signal summoned us to our emergency posts from which we expected to abandon ship and from where we were standing the sea looked a long way down. We didn't have to jump, however, as they must have decided to take us off and a destroyer came alongside and commenced to do this when an announcement was made for all gun crews to return to the guns and this we did, but when we sorted ourselves out we found only half the gunners had returned. The others must have been smarter than us and were off.

The Powers-That-Be must have decided to tow the ship and we were the only defence if the enemy should come back to finish us off. One cheerful sailor told us the water was getting higher and higher and there would be a big bang if it reached the batteries, so we cheered ourselves up by trying to drink the abandoned canteen dry. The tow continued for several hours until it was decided to discontinue the tow as were drifting towards Tunis which was Vichy French and it would have meant internment if we landed there.

Another destroyer, *Oribi*, came to take us off, but we had to remove our guns for transfer to the destroyer. We also had to transfer the deck cargo of sacks of potatoes and then they took us off, whereupon we were confined to the lower deck of the *Oribi* and saw nothing of the sinking of the *Imperial Star*, although we heard all the gunfire and were left in darkness every time they fired. She was the only ship in the convoy to be sunk.

When the *Imperial Star* was finally destroyed the *Oribi* raced all the way to Malta and. We were lucky because having had more time than the others who had abandoned ship earlier we managed to come off with our small kit, whereas the earlier ones had taken nothing.

I found Malta in September a very pleasant place to be, as we could buy things at the NAAFI that had ceased to be available in Britain, but this situation soon changed when the Germans left the Russian Front to set about their efforts to annihilate this little island. And they nearly did too.

I was stationed at RAF Luqa, and for the next eighteen months I was up to my eyes in bombs of all sizes and types, both ours and theirs. At that time there were Blenheims and Wellingtons operating from Luqa and we fed hem bombs from our bomb dump at the end of Safi strip.

The Wellingtons were dispersed at the Siggiewi end of the airfield. Our bomb dump at Luqa was an open area about 300 yards from Kirkop Village which was handy for the dump workers at break time because of big, fat egg sandwiches which could be had from Mary's bar in the village and before food shortages hit the local people.

Corporal 'Jock' Pryde was the bomb tractor driver who used to pull about five loaded trailers, with the delivery staff sitting on the bombs. One day he was given a tractor which was under-powered because it could not pull the load up incline to the airfield beyond the dispersal strip so we unhitched the last trailer and three others and myself stayed to push it to the side of the strip for safety as there was one of 69 Squadron's Marylands taxing up the strip to get to the runway. As it was drawing close to us I could see Jock had unhitched another trailer further up the hill, with nobody in attendance, and it was in the direct path of the approaching Maryland… I made signals for the pilot to stop, but he carried on and seconds later ran into the trailer, which was about thirty yards from us and loaded with four 500 pound bombs. The ensuing explosion threw us down and one of the Maryland's undercarriage legs flew over us and landed close to our trailer Apart from shock I received no injuries but my companions were slightly injured. If I had been a bigger chap I might not have been so lucky. At the ensuing enquiry the inquiring officer, Wing Commander Fowell Sheddon told me, "Our bombs are no good, Hill, you should be dead". Considering four 500 pounders had exploded so close to us I think he may have been right!

The bomb dump at Luqa was not a healthy place when the Jerries were about, but they always adopted the same approach, making their bombing run up Safi Strip, where most of our aircraft were dispersed. They usually went way out East before turning in to make their run so we usually stayed at the dump until we saw them turn towards us then make a quick sprint to the village for shelter. On the day of 29th December 1941 they surprised us by turning in considerably earlier and we had to vacate the dump in great haste. Bombs were falling long before we made it to the village and it became obvious that our dump was today's target.

We had always been welcomed by the village people, but this day they chased us away with stones because the Germans had wrecked parts of the village as well as making a thorough job of destroying our bomb dump. Afterwards when we went to see the ruins we found a biggest bomb crater imaginable where two large stacks of 1,000 bombs had been.

That day we had loaded all the Wellingtons on Safi Strip with bombs for that night's targets but the destruction of our dump caused the nearest dispersed aircraft to explode, which then started a chain of burning aircraft. Only one Wellington survived the destruction and the survivor was shifted onto the airfield to await take-off time. Unfortunately this aircraft was parked close to where, unknown to anyone, the Germans had dropped a delayed-action bomb which had burrowed into the ground. The bomb exploded an hour before take-off time; no ops that night.

Next morning the Station Armament Officer told me there were two bombs still amongst the wreckage and asked me (!) to make them safe. I approached the still hot wreck and set about the doubtful task of removing the detonators. Several 'top brass' types were surveying the wreckage but they made a hasty departure when they spotted Tich Hill playing with fire!

On another occasion my friendly SAO sent me on a similar errand when one of the Wimpeys crashed after take off on a hillside west of Luqa. The aircraft was fully loaded with small containers of 20 and 40lb fragmentation bombs and 4lb incendiaries. When I got to the crash site there were a number of soldiers combing the wreckage, carrying bags in which they put what was left of the crew, but they had to battle with a pack of hungry dogs which had got there first. Into the middle of this I had to extract and make safe the few bombs which had not exploded.

In 1942 the Germans dropped vast quantities of "butterfly bombs". Often these deadly weapons did not explode on impact with the ground and lurked everywhere, often hidden in the grass, waiting for someone to kick them. We had several safe ways of dealing with these little terrors, but one armourer named Corporal Jones had a special way. Cpl Jones treated these bombs with contempt and often said "These bloody things wouldn't blow your hat off." He would pick them up gently with both hands and drop them down the nearest quarry, of which there were plenty. The result was that he did it once too often and it blew more than his hat off; we could only recognise the body by a large birthmark on his leg.

In December 1942 I was promoted sergeant and after a few months and many more incidents with bombs (which had become my pet hate) I became surplus to requirements and was posted to Ta Kali and 272 Squadron (Beaufighters). Hurrah! I thought, no more bombs, only Hispanos, Brownings and cameras. But no! I hadn't been there long before they fitted racks under the wings to carry 250lb bombs, so it was back to the old treadmill. The same happened when they 'lent' me to a Spitfire squadron during the invasion of Sicily – fitting 250-pounders again.

When 272 Squadron moved to Sicily I had to say "farewell" to Malta after serving there for two years, but Malta gave me a final scare before leaving... Anybody who served at Luqa will remember the quarry at the east end of the main runway, where many aircraft perished after overshooting on landing or take-off. A group of us were off to Trapani in Sicily in an old Wimpy that had seen better days. Seated in the fuselage of the Wimpy I could not see out, but as we trundled along the runway I could imagine the quarry getting nearer... At the very last moment the plane seemed to give a leap and we became airborne but an airman who had been watching from the astrodome turned round and said, "We only just made it!"

13. THE DELAYED ARRIVAL OF THE G.C.

Chev. Sqdn. Ldr. Victor Betty K.S.J. – RAF (Rtd)

His Majesty King George VI awarded the George Cross to the island of Malta in April 1942 and charged Lord Gort, the Governor designate, to convey this honour to the people of Malta on taking up office in May of the same year. However, certain details of His Majesty's command were not carried out. If the speeches of Lord Gort are studied it will be realised that on no occasion did he state that he actually brought the George Cross to Malta. In this, of course, he was correct. The true story behind the arrival of the George Cross in Malta is one of administrative error – entirely understandable in those times of stress.

The transport communication route between the UK and Malta was from RAF Hendon via Portreith and Gibraltar. The only aircraft with the necessary range was the Lockheed Hudson so this was used as a transport aircraft. It was small and uncomfortable and had little capacity to keep beyond the range of the German Focke Wulf Condor which patrolled the Western Approaches and the Bay of Biscay. Wisely, it was decided to transport the newly appointed Governor and his staff in a Catalina flying boat from Southampton. This was a much safer route and it proved a more suitable and comfortable aircraft. The Catalina was then the longest range aircraft in service with the RAF.

There appears to have been a lack of communication somewhere in the administrative chain. An assumption had been made that Lord Gort would travel by the usual land-based route from RAF Hendon and the George Cross, together with the citation, was duly sent to Hendon. When the error was discovered, the highly classified package was rushed to Southampton but it arrived too late and the captain of the Catalina, bound by the needs of safety and the hours of darkness, was compelled to take off without it. So the George Cross was left behind and Lord Gort travelled to Malta without the decoration awarded to the island and entrusted to him by the King. One can only imagine his embarrassment.

Lord Gort arrived at night in Kalafrana, the only seaplane or flying boat base available in those days. It is recorded that General Sir William Dobbie, the retiring Governor of Malta, asked Lord Gort if he could see the George Cross (which had been awarded whilst Malta was under his Governorship) but Lord Gort refused. In his memoirs Dobbie recorded that Gort "had it in his pocket". Little did he suspect that the medal was not even in Gort's possession. Gort was a man of the highest integrity but he remained silent. Newspapers and radio jumped to the conclusion that he had indeed discharged His Majesty's command. The error became a myth and was perpetuated.

To remedy the failure to deliver the important package to the flying boat at Southampton on time, the Air Ministry sent it to Malta by the first available "Safe hand of officer". It so occurred that the task was entrusted to a young RAF officer, Flying Officer Victor Betty, who was returning from detachment at RAF Abbotsinch, where he had been helping to prepare and test Spitfire aircraft for loading onto the USS aircraft carrier *Wasp* for transport to Malta. On completion of this duty F/O Betty was ordered to report to the Air Ministry in London where he was entrusted with the George Cross's safe conduct to Malta. He travelled from RAF Hendon via Portreith (Cornwall) and Gibraltar, arriving at RAF Luqa at about 0200 hours on 9th May. He was tired, dirty and not in a very good mood to be met by an immaculate Army subaltern from the Governor's staff, requesting to accept custody of the George Cross. This brash young subaltern at first refused to sign the receipt but was met by the ultimatum "No receipt, no George Cross." He signed.

The pilot of the Lockheed Hudson which conveyed F/O Betty was Flying Officer Honeman, who had previously served with the famous 84 Squadron in 1936.

14. LITTLE SHIPS – BIG TASKS

Leading Signalman E.N. Butcher

I was a signalman RN drafted to the *Queen Elizabeth* after two years on a destroyer, so you can guess my mixed feelings towards C-in-C draft for posting me to a passenger liner instead of another "boat". At least my chances of promotion would be easier; and I was still just 20 years old.

The *Queen Elizabeth* was out in the Med, so I boarded the destroyer *Forrester* in May 1941 as a passenger to Malta and was employed on the Flag Deck throughout the whole voyage. The convoy suffered the usual bombings and sinkings en route and on arrival in the Grand Harbour I was drafted to HMS *St Angelo* to transfer to Alexandria to join the "QE". But unfortunately she had been severely damaged by Italian torpedo boats so my draft was cancelled.

I hoped for a home draft, but no, Malta was short of signalmen so I was shanghaied at St Angelo, where I remained for two months. I volunteered for sea, hoping for a fleet draft, but instead was drafted to the auxiliary minesweeper (tug) *Andromeda* (there was a flotilla of these vessels in Malta). Except for key ratings, the stokers and seamen were all Maltese – and a very brave bunch of lads they were. These vessels have never been mentioned in any of the books about wartime Malta; I don't think their authors knew we existed, although the submarines at Manoel Island surely remember the "Smokey Joes" which tried to sweep the channel clear under appalling conditions; bombed continually in harbour and attacked at sea.

Another convoy arrived, including HMS *Penelope* in a very serious condition, having been attacked several times. The merchant ships *Pampus* and *Talabot* were grounded in Grand Harbour and for days tug duties were ordered and we towed ammunition lighters from the two merchant ships whilst all hell was going on in the Grand Harbour as the Germans tried to sink the "Pepperpot", as she was affectionately known.

With our two Lewis guns and one heavy automatic we blazed helplessly away at the hordes of Stukas whilst we towed the lighters to the dockside. The Maltese crew stood wonderfully firm under the strain and were a credit to their country. One merchantman was still smouldering after being on fire but these brave Maltese lads carried on regardless.

Eventually our luck ran out. A near miss on the "Pepperpot" nearly hit us and the *Andromeda* broke her back. No casualties, thank the Lord, so back to *St Angelo* I went. Here my duties entailed watchkeeping on top of St Angelo, which was in contact by semaphore and flashlight with Castille Signal Station, as most telephones were out of action due to the continual bombing. Maltese Boy Scouts were being used as messengers ashore and a brave lot of lads they were. I think some were only 12 years old.

We were close to a Bofors gun manned by the Army, which at that time was rationed to 20 rounds per day, so bad was our plight. The attacks seemed never ending and were usually carried out by at least 30 Stukas and numerous JU88s.

Food was poor – salad and corned beef, some cheese and three slices of bread a day. Civilians were short of cooking oil and nursing mother's milk dried up owing to their poor diet. HMS *Manxman* and HMS *Welshman* ran the gauntlet to bring in emergency supplies, including powdered milk for the mothers. "Victory Kitchens" were opened by the Governor to try and supply a cheap meal to the very hungry Maltese.

Torpedoes and ammunition brought in by the two fast minelayers gave us a few more weeks to hit back at the enemy.

A funny episode happened one afternoon off watch. We were in the Cavaliers, our sleeping quarters and mess deck, which was well protected under 20 feet of sandstone, when a raid started again on the Grand Harbour, so we trooped out to watch and see if our ammunition supply could surprise Jerry. One of our shipmates had "Malta Gut" and dashed to the "heads", which were situated just outside. He could only have just sat down when three Stukas broke off and came straight at us, obviously going for the Bofors gun above us. You can well imagine us all diving into the shelter of the "Cavalier", which we knew was safe. There were tremendous explosions which blew us into the "Cavalier". I felt the breath dragged out of my lungs and was covered in dust. After a while I got to my feet and someone said "Where is Matey?" We ran outside to find a near miss had destroyed the toilets, but the rest had missed the Bofors and our Signal Staff on watch were OK. We searched for our mate and eventually found him alive, upside down in a gorse bush, with the lavatory seat clamped onto his posterior. He was moaning but unhurt, but try as we could we could not remove the seat. An ambulance was called and I could not help wondering what the doctors and nurses thought of the casualty, bum in the air, surrounded by a wooden seat. What a picture it must have made! After that we had a slice of bread and jam with a cup of tea, then back to duty. One more raid before sunset.

Our Bofors now had 40 rounds per day.

I still wanted to join the Fleet, especially a destroyer or cruiser, so I volunteered again. Guess what? Permission granted. A small ex-fishing drifter converted to Auxiliary Minesweeper – HMS *Trusty*. The skipper was Clarkson RNR in command with a Maltese crew, so I was back again sweeping; the same routine, day and night, sweeping at sea and in the harbour, encountering German E-Boats occasionally at night. The shortage of rations ashore was now desperate; if a convoy did not arrive shortly things would be unbearable for the brave Maltese, whose conditions were worse than war-torn Europe. On 9th May 1942 we were attacked by three E-Boats, which was too much for our small armament. An "F" signal message was sent ("read but do not answer") I think to the trawler *Swona*, which was on a bearing. Although we used a dimmed blue light all guns seemed to be trained our way and tracers lit up the dark night all around us. I was hit in the leg and blown to the deck below where I remained until after the action. A Maltese risked his life to bring me a tourniquet, which I secured, as I was bleeding badly. Afterwards our skipper said my action had probably saved us more serious damage as the "E" Boats retired, knowing reinforcements were near. Being the only signalman on board and still on the deck and unable to get to the bridge I made signals to the *Castille* from the deck and told the coxswain what flags, etc to fly on entering harbour. *Castille* sent ambulance for me, from which I was transferred to hospital, having lost a lot of blood.

Conditions in the hospital were terrible; all the windows were damaged and how doctors and nurses carried on under such primitive conditions I shall never know. Wounded were lying on stretchers awaiting their turn for surgery from various bombing raids that night. The hospital canteen, I was told, was all but empty but sold a few razor blades. Tea with lemon, no sugar or milk, an occasional packet of cigarettes, otherwise we used what paper we could find to roll our own. The bombing was still bad and except for patients in bed it was a case of 'off to the shelter' again. The orderlies covered us under a mattress while the raid was on and stayed with us during the raids. They were the Royal Army Medical Corps and they were great. We were always hungry. We had salad day in and day out, with a little meat and potatoes once a week and sometimes, but not often, a sweet of some kind.

The ward was overflowing with badly wounded and burned casualties and loss of weight was normal. I weighed 11 stone 12 lbs when I arrived in Malta and was now about 9 stone. It turned out that I was very lucky; the *Trusty Star* blew up on a mine three days after my entry into hospital and I never knew for sure how many casualties there were. I was very upset.

August 1942. We heard heavy gunfire from our hospital beds and it turned out to be the 'Pedestal' Convoy ('Santa Maria' Convoy, as the Maltese called it) fighting their way to relieve Malta. As is well known, the convoy got through with the gallant "Ohio" which has been written into many a book of her fighting spirit and the courage of her crew to get through. This was the turning point of the "Great Siege". Rationing increased and saved the island. Germany was beaten. Malta then really turned to the offensive with submarines and bombers. For the first time in 18 months a weight was lifted from the Maltese.

In October I was flown to Gibraltar in a Lockheed Hudson, which even then was the only way for wounded etc to leave Malta. The only other way was by submarine, which took days. We took of from Luqa at 0200 hours in the middle of the night and my last view of Malta was of searchlights and the brave little island hitting back with everything. Still in plaster on my left leg and my weight just over 8 stone, I was unable to leave Gibraltar until I had gained a stone in weight.

Arrived in the UK in December 1942 and left hospital May 1943 after a year in hospital. I was medically discharged from the RN in 1946 due to the leg wound, which never really healed.

I returned to Malta with the George Cross Island Association in 1988 and found the Maltese people pleased to see us; their hospitality was wonderful. I have herewith a list of all the "Smokey Joes", which have been long forgotten and I hope some reference will be made to their memory and the brave Maltese crews.

FLOTILLA OF AUXILIARY MINESWEEPERS – MALTA 1942

Andromeda	Sunk	18 April 1942
Trusty Star	Mined	13 May 1942
Ploughboy	Damaged	March 1942
Sunset	Sunk	01 April 1942
Emily	Sunk	07 March 1942
Eddy	Sunk	26 May 1942
St Angelo	Bombed	May 1942
Girl Margaret	Burnt out	May 1942
Jade	Sunk	21 April 1942
Coral	Sunk	21 April 1942
Abingdon	Sunk	05 April 1942
Permoy	Sunk	04 May 1942

Other small vessels included:[1]

Beryl, Medusa, Lanner, Saha, Swona, Cromarty, Boston, Hebe, Hythe, Rye, Speedy, Whitehaven, Fellowship and *Justified*.

Beryl.

---

[1] Editors Note: I have added the names of the other small ships that were involved and which also must never be forgotten. I know some of those mentioned were also sunk.

15. A Ferry Pilot's Tale

R. Carter – R.A.F

Few people are aware of the early attempts to get up-to-date fighter planes to Malta. Early in the war the RAF was desperately short of aircraft and any aid to the island could not be considered until well into 1940. Then the decision was made to send some Hurricanes, but the problem was how to get them there? The first flight of twelve Hurricanes was to be a trial one and the route, through France to Marseilles and thence via Tunis to Malta was to be made using pilots from the Ferry Pilots Pool. Long range fuel tanks with immersed electric pumps were fitted to the underside of each wing and guns and armour plating were removed to save weight. These would be carried by the twelve Blenheims which were to accompany us and would afterwards be on their way to Egypt.

There were not enough maps to go round, but we were told not to worry as there would be a navigator in one of the Blenheims! I did manage to get hold of a naval chart for part of the Med, which was better than nothing. We had no oxygen and nobody thought of issuing us with tropical kit. Just before we took off we heard the shattering news that France had capitulated, but the message from the Air Ministry was "proceed as best you can".

We travelled in follow-your-leader fashion at reduced speed to allow us a longer range. As we proceeded into France we were hit by cloud and rain so thick we could not see the aircraft immediately in front of us so we became separated. Some climbed to get over the cloud and some went lower and apparently one Blenheim and one Hurricane turned back. I continued climbing to 22,000ft but could not get out of the cloud and with no oxygen soon felt the ill-effects and had to descend to 12,000ft and continue the flight on instruments. When I broke cloud I was relieved to be right on the coast and a few miles from Marseilles. I landed with fuel tanks almost empty, soon followed by a Blenheim and then two more Blenheims and Hurricanes.

We received a cool reception; nobody wanted to take responsibility, but the sight of our loaded revolvers persuaded the ground staff to fill our tanks. Running out of light and not wanting to stay in Marseilles too long we took off for Corsica, where we landed at Calvi. There was some difficulty starting next morning, a back-breaking job using the starting handles, and we had to clear the magneto points on the engine with an old screwdriver, penknife and nail file. On the way to Tunis we saw an Italian aircraft coming towards us but he backed away into the cloud, which was lucky for us. Fortunately he did not know we were unarmed.

I will never forget the sight looking down on Luqa aerodrome where we had been instructed to land in Malta. It was barely recognisable, for it was covered with all sorts of obstructions, trucks, old cars, tractors … and some very fresh bomb craters. We fired the recognition signal of the day, lowered our undercarriages and waited. Suddenly there was a fantastic sight of all the wheeled vehicles moving to one side to give room to land – just two Hurricanes and three Blenheims, with a third Hurricane arriving the next day.

We provided a great boost to the morale of people striving to hold off the attacks of the Axis Powers but the flight proved it was not practical to fly fighters from Britain at that stage of the war. Subsequent deliveries of Hurricanes and Spitfires were made from aircraft carriers or from the Gold Coast where they were shipped in crates, reassembled and then flown across Africa to various Middle East destinations.

16. A Very Brave Pilot

Nat Gold – 830 Squadron FAA, Hal Far

Of course all the pilots who flew in wartime Malta did a splendid job, but there is one particular pilot to whom I would like to pay tribute, a Fulmer pilot from the HMS *Illustrious* named Lt William Lawrence Le Cocq Barnes RN, DSC.

I had just arrived at Hal Far, Malta to join 830 Squadron (after travelling round the Cape and narrowly avoiding being torpedoed in the Med) with three other TAGs: Alan Todd, S.S. Clark and Bill Thomson. The date was 10th January 1941, the day the *Illustrious* received a terrible pounding. We stood on the drome at Hal Far and witnessed a sickening sight. Out at sea we could see *Illustrious* on fire, listing and desperately trying to limp into Grand Harbour. It was even more sickening for Toddy and me, remembering that we had been drafted to HQ on board the *Illustrious*, but both fell ill with "Gyppo" tummy. The TAG who took my place (R.N.S.R. Course, Worthy Down) and to whom I owed 10 Piasters, we heard later that he had been put on flying duties because of the emergency and whilst sitting in his Fulmer on the after lift a bomb had landed on top of him.

Illustrious did make harbour, but Jerry wouldn't let her rest; a large plot of German Aircraft were coming in to try and finish her off.

All the ships and harbour defence guns were elevated upwards and commenced a devastating box barrage. Looking across towards the Grand Harbour from Hal Far we could hear the Pom-Poms sounding their Chicago Orchestration and the Bofors their regular boom-boom-boom. Undeterred Jerry dived through the barrage, but at Hal Far there was one *Illustrious* Pilot (the aforementioned Lt William Lawrence Le Cocq Barnes) who, it seemed, wanted to get his own revenge on what Jerry had done to his ship and comrades. There were no other fighters to assist the ground defences so this lone lieutenant took off in his Fulmer, with no observer or TAG. Gaining height he flew towards Grand Harbour then, circling, he suddenly pounced like a spider in its web and followed the next German aircraft to dive down through that terrible barrage as Jerry released his lethal load and pulled out the Lieutenant picked him off.

Ammunition spent, the Lieutenant flew back to Hal Far to re-arm. He taxied up to the tarmac, pushed the cockpit cover back, removed his helmet and put on his peaked cap. Whilst the armourers were frantically falling over themselves the lieutenant, of medium height and wearing his Mae West, paced up and down, drawing deeply on a cigarette and deep in thought. When the armourers completed their task the lieutenant almost dived into the cockpit; he couldn't get airborne fast enough and take off was rather erratic.

Again we witnessed the same tactics, diving down through the barrage on the tail of another German and again he returned for rearming and paced up and down like a wild cat whilst drawing deeply on another cigarette. Airborne again, he went back and carried on where he had left off. How many times he got his revenge I do not know, but he came back safely and unscathed. How he got away with it, only God knows.

A week later this Lieutenant, whilst travelling with Commander Flying of the *Illustrious* in an old box type ford saloon were challenged by a Maltese sentry. It seems the chauffeur did not hear, the sentry took aim and fired at the car, he missed, but the bullet hit a rock and ricocheted off, piercing the rear of the car hitting the Lieutenant in the back and killing him instantly. We were all stunned and just could not believe what had happened. If thoughts could kill, that sentry would have been a dead man.

17. FAITH, HOPE & CHARITY

Sgt H.J Randall – RAF

In May 1940 the C-in-C Mediterranean, at the request of the AOC Malta, agreed to the loan of three Sea Gladiators which were in store in Kalafrana, for the purpose of forming a local fighter defence unit. A fighter flight comprising these aircraft, with six pilots drawn from local RAF resources, was duly formed at Hal Far on 4th June 1940 after a month's training of pilots, none of whom had previous experience of fighter aircraft, or methods of operations.

Italy declared war on 11th June 1940 and at 0645 hours on that day Faith, Hope and Charity were airborne on their first operational flight, which was to intercept ten Italian SM79s attacking the dockyard and Hal Far aerodrome; the enemy aircraft were driven off. During the evening of the same day, Faith, Hope and Charity took off to intercept 25 enemy bombers approaching the island and shot down one of them without loss to themselves.

For the next 18 days these Gladiators were airborne at least once a day and took on, single-handed, a total of 144 enemy bombers and their fighter escorts. The Italians at first underestimated the Gladiators and sent over their bombers unescorted, but from the 16th onwards they began to use Macchi 200s as escorts. This did not prevent the Gladiators from driving off the raiders and by the end of this period they had destroyed or damaged five enemy aircraft without loss to themselves.

By the 28th June Malta fighter strength had been increased by the addition of four Hurricanes which, while on passage from UK to Egypt, were retained in Malta by the permission of the AOC-in-C Middle East. The Gladiators, however, continued to operate and whether flying by themselves or with the more modern Hurricanes made repeated interceptions of enemy aircraft attacking the island. On 10th July, for example, three out of a total of 20 raiders were shot down and damage amounted to no more than 20 goats killed and one bull.

On 31st July, Faith, Hope and Charity were despatched to intercept one bomber strongly escorted by nine enemy fighters. One enemy fighter was shot down and the remainder fled. On 17th September, together with three Hurricanes, they took on a formation of 12 JU87s escorted by 25 CR42s; two of the JU87s and 1 CR42 were destroyed.

The last time Faith, Hope and Charity were airborne was on 12th November, when a formation of Macchi 200s attempted to machine gun Luqa. Again the Gladiators intercepted and one Macchi 200 was shot down.

During these five months the Gladiators had played a great part in defending Malta and together with the Hurricanes had made 72 interceptions in which 37 enemy aircraft were destroyed or damaged. By this time Charity had been destroyed and Hope damaged but our Hurricane strength had increased and it was thus possible for Faith to go into honourable retirement.

A Gloster Gladiator – One of the three, Faith Hope and Charity

18.   *USS WASP* TO THE RESCUE!

Chuck Stoat

For more than two years following the outbreak of World War Two in September 1939, Britain, with aid from her Commonwealth countries, was the sole barrier between a free world and Nazi domination. Unprepared for war, British forces sustained tremendous losses on land, sea and in the air and thousands of civilians fell victim to Luftwaffe attacks on the populated areas of Britain, to say nothing of the carnage suffered by the citizens of Belgium, Denmark, Holland, France, Norway, Poland and other nations as the Nazis blitzkrieged their way across Europe.

The British Army suffered a stunning defeat in France and Belgium, and was facing annihilation. It was solely as a result of Hitler's decision to parade his armoured divisions through Paris that the British Expeditionary Force of over 330,000 men was able to be rescued during what was to become known as "The Miracle at Dunkirk". The Royal Navy was stretched to its limit in the Atlantic and Pacific oceans and the Mediterranean. Included among its many losses during that period was the battle cruiser HMS *Hood*, the largest warship in the world in 1939. The vessel was sunk on 24th May 1940 by a salvo from the mighty German battleship *Bismarck*. Only three of the Hood's crew of 1,477 survived.

Another very significant loss was HMS *Ark Royal*, the most famous aircraft carrier in the Royal Navy. Among the vessel's claims to fame were her involvement in the sinking of the *Bismarck* and her actions in the Mediterranean that included escorting two supply convoys to Malta and, on four occasions, the conveyance of reinforcement aircraft to the besieged island. It was on return from the fourth delivery that *Ark Royal* was torpedoed and sunk on 13th November 1941 by the German submarine U-81 when the carrier was only 30 miles from Gibraltar, her destination. Unlike the *Hood*, however, all of her crew survived but one.

The Royal Air Force fared no better during the early years of the war but, of course, will always be remembered as victors of "The Battle of Britain". The RAF also experienced tremendous losses in France and Belgium prior to the Dunkirk evacuation. Soon they would be stretched to their limit in North Africa and were about to fight an almost hopeless battle in defence of Malta.

On 10th June 1940 Benito Mussolini declared war on Britain and France and the following day the Italian air force carried out its first raid on Malta. This tiny island of only 120 square miles, located in the Mediterranean just 60 miles south of Sicily and about 110 miles east of Tunisia, was of great strategic importance to both Britain and the Axis powers. Mussolini's goal of building a new Roman Empire in North Africa that would dominate the Mediterranean, with himself as the modern-day Caesar, had begun prior to Italy's declaration of war when he assigned 215,000 troops and 280 aircraft to the Italian colony of Libya that was bordered on the west by French Tunisia. However, with France's capitulation to German forces in June 1940, the threat from Tunisia was no longer a concern and the Italian troops and aircraft were reassembled near Libya's eastern border with Egypt, which at that time was under British protection.

Britain's main interests in the Middle East were the defence of Egypt, the Suez Canal and in the rich oil supply of the Persian Gulf, but in June 1940 RAF Middle East Air Command (MEAC) had only 300 aircraft on strength to defend more than 4.5 million square miles of territory that ran west to east from Egypt to Iraq and north to south from Greece and the Balkans to Ethiopia and Kenya. The majority of these 300 aircraft were outdated, with almost 50% of the total based in Egypt. It is reported that Malta was the worst-equipped RAF outpost in the Middle East. Four squadrons of Hurricanes promised for the defence of the island never arrived prior to Mussolini's first attack on 11th June 1940. As a result, only three Gloster Gladiators were at hand to defend the island, and although obsolete, one managed to down a Macchi-Castoldi 200 while the rest of the raiders were turned back to sea.

By the end of June, four hurricanes arrived to join the three Gladiators at Malta. A further twelve of the type arrived in August which were almost immediately followed by a number of twin-engined Blenheim bombers. The latter aircraft began striking enemy airfields, ports and communication lines in an attempt to disrupt the Italian offensive against the British in the North African desert.

The results were initially positive when the British forces closed an 80 mile gap in the front lines on 7th December 1940. Over the next two months, they pushed on a further 500 miles into Libya, during which time they routed nine Italian divisions and captured some 130,000 prisoners. RAF bomber squadrons from both Malta and the Suez Canal area, by their constant strikes against the enemy supply lines, had played a significant role in the British army's early successes in the desert. But now Britain's worst fears were realized. Hitler had tired of the Italian efforts in attempting to defeat the British in the North African desert and deployed an armoured force to Tripoli on 12th February 1941. Six weeks later, the German 'Africa Korps' began their offensive, under the command of General Erwin Rommel, soon to become notorious as "the Desert Fox".

In Eastern Europe on 6th April 1941 German forces crossed the Bulgarian frontier and proceeded south towards Greece and the island of Crete in support of their Italian allies. By May 31st both Greece and Crete were under Axis occupation. One positive note was that 15,000 British soldiers were successfully evacuated from Crete.

With Rommel now routing her forces in the North African desert, Britain's only hope was the RAF squadrons based on the island of Malta. If they could cut off the enemy's supply routes across the Mediterranean there was a good possibility that Rommel's mechanized troops could be halted. Another squadron of Blenheims was assigned to the island in June 1941 solely for that purpose.

The summer of 1941 saw an increase in Middle East Command to 51 squadrons, most of which were in North Africa. The outdated Gladiators in the desert were replaced by newly-acquired Curtiss Tomahawks and Kittyhawks. These were the first of the type to be adorned with the famous 'shark's mouth' that was eventually to become the trademark of the American Volunteer Group, the Flying Tigers. As well, the earlier Mk.1 Hurricanes were replaced by Mk.IIs, but these were still no match for the German Messerschmitt Me109F.

On Malta, Spitfires were beginning to arrive by sea in small batches. Bomber squadrons now included twin-engined Blenheims, Wellingtons and Baltimores, which accounted for some 100,000 tons of Axis shipping sunk between the months of May and October. But the Luftwaffe was not idle and it was becoming more and more of a problem in transporting vital supplies to the island as its Ju87 'Stukas' and other types took their toll on Allied shipping.

A major British offensive was mounted on 18th November 1941 but soon faltered, turning instead into a see-saw battle of thrusts and counter-thrusts. By early December both the British and German forces in the North African desert were exhausted and running short of supplies, resulting in the easing of hostilities for a brief period. But the situation was about to change...

On 7th December 1941 Japanese forces attacked Pearl Harbour and British possessions in Asia the following day. As a result, aircraft that had originally been assigned to RAF units in North Africa and Malta were immediately diverted to the Far East. However, vital assistance had been supplied to Malta earlier by Royal Navy Fleet Air Arm Swordfish and Albacore squadrons who by the end of the year had destroyed some 400,000 tons of enemy shipping.

In January 1942, the battle was resumed by Rommel's forces following the safe arrival of an Axis supply convoy at Tripoli. The Luftwaffe squadrons based in Sicily began continuous bombing and anti-shipping strikes on and around the tiny island of Malta, with the result that defending RAF fighter strength was severely reduced. Owing to the distances involved and Luftwaffe interceptions, the supply of replacement aircraft was almost impossible either overland, by ferry delivery or by sea.

Not only the RAF was suffering. The effective German supply blockade had brought the Maltese almost to the point of starvation. A few ships in convoys managed to sail as far as the island but were almost invariably sunk by German attackers before they could unload their precious cargoes. By February the RAF on Malta had no alternative but to divert their twin-engined bombers to Egypt and comparative safety. Needless to say, British airfields were prime targets and the few that existed on the island were under constant attack. As an indication of the Luftwaffe's determination to eliminate the RAF threat to their marine supply lines, almost 11,000 enemy sorties were flown against Malta during the thirteen-week period between February 25 and May 25. This total was split almost evenly between fighter and bomber types.

Britain's Prime Minister Winston Churchill was greatly concerned with the Malta crisis but was determined to maintain the island in British hands. A small number of Spitfires equipped with long-range 90 gallon ferry tanks had been delivered, sixteen at a time, on a few occasions by HMS *Eagle* which at the time was the largest carrier in Royal Navy service. When within 600 miles of the island they were flown from the carrier's deck to begin their long and hazardous flight to Malta. But these arrivals, although most welcome, were far too few and were inevitability lost within a few days of their receipt. What the Malta-based RAF squadrons required was a large one-time delivery of Spitfires if they were to effectively challenge the attacking Luftwaffe. By late March, however, even the small deliveries had to he postponed when HMS *Eagle* was withdrawn from service for repair. At that time 200 Italian and 400 German fighters were assembled in Sicily while the RAF on Malta could muster less than thirty serviceable defenders.

On 1st April 1942 Churchill sent a personal telegram to President Roosevelt outlining the dire circumstances existing on Malta and requested specific assistance in the form of the aircraft carrier USS *Wasp*. This new carrier could accommodate up to 50 Spitfires on one sailing to the island and Churchill advised that this number of defensive aircraft arriving at one time could well turn the tide on the Luftwaffe. Roosevelt agreed to the request three days later.

Ordered in 1935 the USS *Wasp* (OV7) was based on the lightweight and lightly armoured USS *Ranger* launched in 1933. A number of improvements over the latter were incorporated in *Wasp's* design. Rather than the six boilers exhausting (3 on either side of the deck near the rear of the ship) to the atmosphere as on the *Ranger* the boilers on *Wasp* were combined in one funnel. Internal sub-division was improved and structural integrity was increased with the installation of additional bulkheads. The *Wasp's* beam of 80 ft 9 inches was a slight increase over the *Ranger* while her length was reduced by 40 feet.

Propulsion was supplied by e-shaft geared steam turbines developing a total of 75,000 shp. This was an increase of 21,500 shp over that of the *Ranger* and was necessary due to the shorter and wider hull, to attain the designed speed of 29.5 knots. This increase in power was at a cost, however, as it meant an increase in fuel requirements as well.

Wasp's armour consisted of only 1-inch thick steel plating on the deck and a narrow 2-inch thick belt at the waterline. Aircraft movement from the deck to the hangar below was provided by two main inboard elevators with one smaller unit at the edge of the flight deck. The *Wasp* was fitted with three aircraft catapults, two of which were flush-mounted with the forward flight deck while the third, in the hangar deck below, was mounted beam-wise to facilitate launching scout aircraft through either side of the vessel.

The USS *Wasp* displaced 14,700 tons 'empty' and 20,500 tons fully loaded, and could accommodate up to 80 aircraft. Flight deck length was 741 feet 3inches with a width of 109 feet. Defensive armament consisted of eight 5-inch (127mm), sixteen 1.1-inch (28mm) and thirty .79-inch (20mm) cannon. The aircraft carrier was manned by a crew of 2,367 men.

Construction of USS *Wasp* was begun at the Bethlehem Steel Yards in Quincy, Massachusetts in April 1935 and was launched three years later on April 4 1939. The vessel, commissioned on April 25, 1940, was completed by the autumn and immediately began conducting neutrality patrols in the Atlantic. Following the US declaration of War against Japan on December 7, 1941 the *Wasp* remained in the Atlantic, training naval aircrew, until early April 1942 when she was ordered to proceed to Scotland for service with the British Home Fleet.

One British WWII service that has never received its highly merited recognition was the Air Transport Auxiliary (ATA). This group of volunteer men and women delivered military aircraft throughout the British Isles, either new to squadrons from the factories or from squadrons to the Maintenance Units for servicing, thus leaving RAF pilots free to perform their operational duties. After D-Day, the ATA expanded their area of operations to bases on the European continent and into North Africa. All ATA flying personnel were volunteers and many, who, although all were licensed pilots or flight engineers, were either medically or physically unable to meet RAF aircrew standards. At least three members had only one arm, one of these over 50 years of age, and only one eye as well, many wore corrective lenses and many others were supposedly "well past their prime". And, of course, women, regardless of their qualifications, were barred from serving in the RAF as aircrew.

The initials ATA were often the subject of differing interpretations, not all of which were complimentary, but one reputedly coined by a Fleet

Street reporter was perhaps the most appropriate and one which most members of the ATA were quick to adopt unofficially: "Ancient and Tattered Aviators". Though many of their number may well have been, they nevertheless provided a vital service and established an aircraft movement record that will go down in aviation history as second to none. Though non-combative their duties included flying in conditions seldom if ever expected of other branches of the services. Add to that the fact they were given a small page of notes listing the minimum of information on the performance of the aircraft type they were assigned to fly (often for the first time) and then sent off with out the benefit of even a test or familiarization flight and you will begin to understand what an extraordinary bunch of aviators they were.

In 1942, No.4 Ferry Pool ATA was headquartered at Prestwick, Scotland under Commander James McGuinness, a veteran of WWI who had served first as an air gunner and then as a sergeant pilot in the Royal Flying Corps. He remained in the RAF after the war and earned the distinction of being the first non-commissioned pilot in the RAF to receive a commission during peacetime. For a period in the 1920s he served with No.55 Squadron in Baghdad. McGuinness took his discharge in 1935 following twenty years of service, after which he earned both his civil pilot and instructor licences and then served as a flying instructor at the North Staffordshire Flying Club at Meir until joining the ATA shortly after its formation in late 1939.

On 5th April 1942 Commander McGuinness was advised of a Priority One (P1) Spitfire movement and was instructed to act as the Liaison Officer on behalf of the ATA, which was to be involved in the critical transfer due to take place immediately in the area of the River Clyde. The following evening the first six Mark VC Spitfires arrived at Prestwick for delivery to Abbotsinch by No.4 Ferry Pool pilots. Each aircraft was equipped with both a 90 Imperial gallon long-range ferry drop tank, positioned under the centre of the wing and a large, flared Vokes tropical air filter under the nose. Armament consisted of four 20mm cannons.

The next morning Commander McGuinness flew an ATA Fairchild 24 Argus to inspect the conditions at Abbotsinch. Upon arrival over the field he noted the grass was inundated with water and realized that landing Spitfires would be a hazardous undertaking at best. Following a successful, albeit wet, landing he met a number of officers including Sqn Ldr 'Shorty" Hughes, senior engineering officer in charge of the crews tasked with maintaining the aircraft during the transfer. The officers then inspected the airfield on foot, after which they were all in agreement that conditions were far from satisfactory. McGuinness also expressed his opinion that they should be prepared for accidents and possible aircraft losses. To add to the problem, a low front was firmly entrenched in the area providing an unwanted low ceiling and steady drizzle. The Spitfires of Nos 601 and 603 Squadrons were being flown to Prestwick from Brize Norton, Colerne and Little Rissington by ferry pilots from other ATA pools and McGuinness was continually updated on the exact location of each aircraft involved in the transfer.

As time was a most critical factor, No 4 Ferry Pool pilots at Prestwick, who had already been advised of the conditions to be expected, were informed of the decision to ferry the first aircraft to Abbotsinch. Special instructions to the pilots were simply to switch off their engines on touch-down, as taxiing would be impossible. As well, flaps were to be left in the down position to facilitate the removal of mud and other debris prior to their retraction. The first aircraft to arrive was being flown by First Officer Nathan S. Kohn, closely followed by F/O Nicholas G, Pickard and F/O Alexander H. Chase. All three Spitfires were completely enveloped in a sea of mud and water upon touchdown but came to a halt undamaged. Maintenance personnel immediately pushed the aircraft over sheets of corrugated steel to the Tarmac.

In the meantime, Kohn was flown back to Prestwick by an ATA 'taxi' to collect another Spitfire. Following his second successful landing of the day at 15:00 hours, officials made the decision not to risk any further deliveries on April 7th. Although a favourable wind had been forecast for that evening, it did not materialize and adverse conditions remained the same the following day, when only one Spitfire was delivered by Flight Captain Edwin E. Hearing, who had flown direct to Abbotsinch from Brize Norton. It was on this date that personnel involved in the transfer learned that an unidentified aircraft carrier would be anchoring at Greenock, where the Spitfires would be loaded on board. Rumours were also circulating that the vessel would be transporting the fighters into the Mediterranean.

The original plan was to load the aircraft on barges positioned on the River Cart at Abbotsinch then float them to Greenock via the River Clyde for transfer to the carrier anchored in mid stream. Due to the tidal Cart, however, it was realized that only two hours during high tide would be available for the operation. This method therefore had to be cancelled as officials were advised the time the carrier could rein at Greenock was severely limited. Authorities decided the only possible means the transfer could be completed on time would be from a proper docking facility and requested the vessel be moved to nearby Glasgow. Permission was granted and the carrier sailed for the King George V Dock in that city. During this period, one Spitfire was manhandled through the mud to the far end of the Abbotsinch field, where it was loaded onto road transport for conveyance to Glasgow. A trial run was carried out but it was soon realised that the volume of traffic in the town of Paisley would prevent any large aircraft movement in time for the carrier to meet its scheduled departure. Another possibility presented itself when it was noted the town of Renfrew had a small airstrip that would position the aircraft much closer to the docks at Glasgow. Enquiries were made into the feasibility of ferrying the fighters into the tiny strip but the same reply was received from all contacted who were unanimous in replying that the field was far too small to accommodate a Spitfire landing.

Although the weather forecasters were still predicting favourable winds to assist in drying out the field, conditions remained the same. Nevertheless, on April 9, six more Spitfires were safely landed at Abbotsinch but, as each landing became more hazardous, authorities had no choice but to declare the field unserviceable following the sixth arrival. Meanwhile, Spitfires were continually arriving at Prestwick and a survey was conducted to determine if the aircraft could be transferred to Glasgow by road but this alternative was also deemed impossible in the limited time available. The situation had now become desperate. With aircraft on the unserviceable field at Abbotsinch and others thirty to forty miles away at Prestwick, and the carrier en route to Glasgow with a scheduled departure in three days, it was decided the only possible solution was the tiny field at Renfrew – and the outcome depended entirely on the ability of the ATA pilots in landing the high performance aircraft on the small strip.

Tension was very high on the morning of April 10 when the first three Spitfires arrived over the field. Following two or three circuits to assess the conditions, the first pilot to land throttled back, lowered the undercarriage and performed a perfect USS *Wasp* flight deck prior to launching Wildcats to provide air cover during Spitfire launch, landing with the other two accomplishing the same results. On that day, a total of twenty-three Spitfires were safely delivered to the field. On April 11th eight more were received and on the 12th a further ten without incident. The ATA pilots had certainly proven their capabilities. When the order was given to ferry the aircraft to Renfrew, maintenance personnel and their equipment were immediately relocated from Abbotsinch to the tiny field. Concentration now had to be aimed at the means of transferring the Spitfires to the docks in Glasgow. At this time, the RAF had begun ferrying Lockheed Hudsons across the Atlantic. Tex Nixon, a Lockheed Aircraft representative who presumably was in Scotland to monitor the arrival of the

Hudsons, was at Glasgow and assisted in the design and construction of special cradles for installation on six "Queen Marys" (long flatbeds) which would be used to transfer the aircraft to the docks.

Each Spitfire had to be positioned on the flatbed in such a way as to clear roadblock obstructions such as overhead wiring and tramway cables along the chosen route. Both wing tips on each aircraft were removed and deposited in the cockpit to facilitate passage through the narrow streets. Upon arrival the Spitfires would be immediately hoisted on board the carrier flight deck. Once initial problems had been overcome during the first convoy of six aircraft, officials were certain the time limit could be met. Although the whole operation was top secret, the entire transfer was under the close scrutiny of local citizens, many of whom stayed for hours to witness the spectacle.

Maximum effort was expended by RAF ground crewmen to assure the carrier would sail on time. Minor snags encountered were of little concern as these would be rectified by the previously noted maintenance crews, under the command of S/L "Shorty" Hughes, who were scheduled to sail with the vessel.

Fifty-four Spitfires were delivered to Renfrew with a total of forty-seven being loaded on board the carrier. The remaining seven aircraft were flown back to Prestwick for re-allotment. During the entire Spitfire movement, none of the aircraft were damaged and the only incident recorded was of one ferry pilot performing a successful forced landing in a farmer's field while en route to Prestwick. The Spitfire was later flown from the field direct to Renfrew by F/O Pickard.

Special mention must be made of the same F/O N.G. Pickard and F/O E.E. Heering, who ferried 17 and 13 aircraft respectively to Renfrew during this transfer. F/O Pickard, a US citizen who coincidentally had worked on the carrier in the US prior to joining the ATA, recognized the vessel at Glasgow – the first involved to identify it as USS *Wasp*.

All concerned were aware of its identity when *Wasp* sailed on April 13th on schedule for the Mediterranean with its vital load of Spitfires to play its role in Operation 'Calendar'. It was also common knowledge that the aircraft, once the *Wasp* was within range, were to be flown from its deck to the besieged island of Malta.

Prior to the *Wasp*'s arrival at Glasgow, her entire complement of dive and torpedo bombers was flown to bases in Scotland, leaving more available space for the Spitfires to be stored in the hangar deck below. One squadron of Grumman Wildcats was retained on board for self-defence and were to remain on the flight deck during the delivery. As hangar deck space was at a premium, a number of the Spitfires, with gear retracted, wingtips re-installed and maintenance performed, were lashed to the hangar ceiling on straps to accommodate other aircraft on the floor below.

During the night of April 18-19 the convoy passed through the Straits of Gibraltar and steamed full speed for a position about 50 miles north of Algiers, where the Spitfires would be launched the morning of April 20. Shortly after dawn, the first twelve Spitfires were raised on the elevator from the hangar deck below and positioned on the after flight deck. This permitted the aircraft hung from the ceiling to be lowered to the deck, where last-minute checks were performed.

Because of weight restrictions only two of the four 20mm cannons on each Spitfire were loaded with 60 rounds – less than half their full capacity – while the other two remained empty. A toothbrush and paste plus a razor with a few blades and perhaps most important a change of underwear should the enemy be encountered en route (!) were about all each pilot was allowed as a 10lb weight restriction was placed on personal belongings.

With a "runway" of only 741 feet maximum, the fuel-laden Spitfires, designed for land-based operations, would require all the assistance they could get to successfully take off from *Wasp*'s deck. This dictated it would be necessary for the carrier to sail at full speed straight into whatever wind was available.

Aware the *Wasp* was in jeopardy of being spotted and then attacked by Algerian-based enemy bombers, the launch had to be completed in as little time as possible. A number of the *Wasp*'s Wildcats was first sent aloft to provide protection in the event of such an attack. Immediately after the last Wildcat began its takeoff run the first of the twelve Spitfires positioned at the rear of the flight deck was launched. As quickly as possible, the remaining eleven departed, one after another. Meanwhile in the hangar below, the pilot in the Spitfire nearest to the elevator had started his engine and was awaiting the last on-deck Spitfire to depart. As soon as this occurred the elevator descended and the waiting aircraft was taxied onto the elevator which was then raised. The moment the elevator ceased its upward travel the Spitfire was taxied onto the flight deck and the elevator was then immediately lowered for another Spitfire waiting below with its engine now also running.

In the meantime, the pilot in the Spitfire that had just been raised was sitting with brakes on awaiting the chequered flag from the deck officer. When it fell, he advanced the throttle to maximum and began his takeoff run just as the second Spitfire arrived from the hangar deck below. And so it went until all remaining thirty-five aircraft had departed. The orbiting Wildcats were immediately recovered and the *Wasp* and its escort turned west for Gibraltar.

One of the forty-seven Spitfires delivered into the Mediterranean by the *Wasp* was lost at sea while the remaining forty-six arrived safely at Malta only to be destroyed, for the most part, in the fierce fighting that followed during the next few days.

Churchill was well aware of the losses on the island and, never one to pass up an opportunity, contacted Roosevelt for the use of the *Wasp* for a second delivery. Permission was granted and the *Wasp* sailed once more for Glasgow. Discussion of the transfer among ATA members had hardly died down when Commander McGuinness was advised by ATA head-quarters on April 25 of yet another P-1 Spitfire movement that was to begin the following day.

Once again McGuinness proceeded to Renfrew where he met the same officers involved in the previous transfer. All were prepared when the first twelve Spitfires arrived at Prestwick on April 26 with seven of these ferried on to Renfrew the same day. As RAF ground crewmen were not scheduled to arrive at Renfrew until the next morning, the remaining five aircraft were kept overnight at Prestwick.

The following day, the newly-arrived ground crews received an additional thirteen more Spitfires at Renfrew with another ten arriving on April 28. Owing to limited dispersal and the possibility of enemy air attack in the Clyde area the decision was made not to risk ferrying any more to Renfrew until the twenty three Spitfires already on the ground had been transferred to the docks in Glasgow.

The carrier arrived at the King George V Docks on April 29 and ex-citement ran high among ATA personnel involved when they learned it was the *Wasp* once again. During several visits to the vessel, information was gleaned from US Navy crewmen that all Spitfires aboard the first sailing had taken off successfully for Malta (*Wasp* crewmen were unaware that one of the aircraft had been lost en route).

Up to this point, favourable wind direction had been enjoyed at the tiny field in Renfrew, however a change in the weather was forecast on April 29. With only one strip available, the forecast predicted a crosswind that would make landing Spitfires extremely difficult if not impossible. Commander McGuinness reported the predicted change to the authorities and expressed his opinion that it would be advisable to ferry all aircraft assembled on the field at Prestwick to Renfrew immediately. The authorities reluctantly agreed, knowing the Spitfires would be parked in a much closer dispersal and would be running the risk of being destroyed should an enemy air attack occur.

On April 29 twenty Spitfires were safely delivered at Renfrew with one each on April 30 and May 1 for a total of 52 aircraft, which constituted 100% of the complement assigned for the second delivery by the USS *Wasp* to Malta. Road transfer of these Spitfires to the docks went without a hitch as a result of previous experience. An example of the efforts expended by the ground crews is well illustrated by their handling of the last aircraft to arrive at Renfrew on May 1. Immediately after the engine stopped and with the ATA ferry pilot still in the cockpit, all radio, electrical and weapons systems plus engine and airframe were inspected by related tradesmen. Fuel tanks were drained, leaving only enough for the pilot to taxi the Spitfire to the 'Queen Mary' loading point where surplus fuel was then completely drained. The wingtips were removed and deposited in the cockpit to be re-installed on board the *Wasp* after she sailed. The aircraft was then positioned on the special cradle, after which it was transported the 2-3 miles to the docks and then hoisted on board the *Wasp's* flight deck. All of the preceding was accomplished within one hour of the Spitfire's arrival at Renfrew!

Upon receipt of this aircraft, the *Wasp* immediately sailed for the Mediterranean. Meanwhile, the British aircraft carrier HMS *Eagle* had been repaired and arrived at Gibraltar, where seventeen Spitfires were taken on board. She joined the *Wasp* and its convoy as it cleared Gibraltar eastbound on the US carrier's second delivery to Malta under the codename Operation 'Bowery'.

All Spitfires previously delivered to Malta were painted in the desert camouflage pattern of yellow and brown (sand and stone). This worked fine over the desert but was highly conspicuous when observed from above while flying over water. At the request of the RAF in Malta the aircraft involved in the second delivery, plus all future deliveries, were painted in the north European temperate sea scheme of dark green and dark sea grey.

The carriers launched their loads of Spitfires in the early morning hours of May 9. One pilot was killed when his aircraft crashed into the sea following take off. Another Spitfire experienced ferry tank fuel feed problems immediately upon takeoff. The pilot, P/O Smith, circled the vessel while waiting for the last of the Spitfires to depart then safely landed his aircraft on the carrier deck. With no arrester hook, no previous carrier landing experience, and only 741 feet of "runway", it was a most admirable performance. Following repair to the fuel system, Smith departed once again for Malta. Two other Spitfires were lost en route to the island but the remainder arrived safely and proved sufficient to reverse the tide in favour of the RAF at Malta.

In a personal account written in 1945 of No.4 Ferry Pool's involvement in the Spitfire transfer, Commander James McGuinness closed with the following paragraphs:

"Prior to the aircraft carrier sailing, I had the pleasure of seeing over this magnificent ship. Her own aircraft were placed on the flying deck while, in the hangar, Spitfires were lashed to the ceiling with wheels retracted and the floor of the hangar was packed with Spitfires. The same keenness prevailed on board. Our American Allies were all out to see this job through and they were full of stories of the RAF on the first trip which was so successful and were even more sure that the second run would be better. They also had previous experience and we all hoped it would go well on the second run. The carrier sailed again to schedule on 1st May 1942, a really magnificent performance, and it is little wonder that our Prime Minister Mr Churchill made the remark in the House of Commons "Who said a Wasp cannot sting twice?" This was the Wasp that stung twice when over 99 Spitfires were delivered to Malta in so short a period. This was the turn of the tide for Malta, a turn of the tide in the Mediterranean, a turn of the tide for North Africa and we all know what has followed."

Immediately after the last Spitfire was launched, the USS *Wasp* headed west for Gibraltar then on to Scotland, where it retrieved its complement of torpedo and dive bombers, after which she proceeded to Norfolk, Virginia. Following replenishment she sailed through the Panama Canal on 10th June 1942 bound for San Diego and, on July 1st departed the California naval base escorting a convoy bound for New Zealand and Guadalcanal. *Wasp* conducted her first combat mission on August 7th when sixteen F4F Wildcat fighters and fifteen SBD Dauntless dive bombers were launched. On this and the following day, over 300 sorties were flown in support of the US Marine invasion of Tulagi and two smaller nearby islands.

As a direct result of losing both *Lexington* and *Yorkton* during the Battle of Midway in June, Admiral Fletcher, commander of the carriers *Enterprise*, *Saratoga* and *Wasp*, which were accompanying Admiral Nimitz's Pacific Fleet, had previously announced he would not maintain his aircraft carriers on station for more than forty-eight hours at a time during the invasions of Guadalcanal and Tulagi. True to his word, participating carriers were withdrawn from the invasion fleet and sailed south-eastward following recovery of their aircraft on August 8.

On the evening of August 3, Admiral Fletcher ordered the *Wasp* and its support ships to Noumea, New Caledonia, for refuelling. This was a reprieve for the *Wasp* as Fletcher was, of course, unaware that the Battle of the Eastern Solomons would begin the following morning. On August 24, the *Enterprise* was attacked by Japanese carrier-based aircraft and severely damaged, resulting in her being sent to Hawaii for repairs.

On August 31 *Saratoga* was hit by one of six torpedoes fired by the Japanese submarine 1-26. Although only minor damage was inflicted, she too was withdrawn and sailed for Tongatabu near the Fiji Islands for repair. Meanwhile at Noumea the *Wasp* embarked USMC fighters for transfer to Guadalcanal for which she sailed on September 13. The newly built USS *Hornet*, just recently arrived from Pearl Harbour following training operations, was the only carrier there to greet her when she arrived on station. Shortly after dawn on September 15, the *Wasp* had just finished flying off her load of fighters when lookouts noted four torpedo wakes approaching the carrier. Since this article was originally published in *Air Classics* the author has learned from a *Wasp* crewman on board at the time that the wakes were at first thought to be trails from 'escorting' dolphins! In fact, the Japanese-submarine 1-19 had managed to penetrate the *Wasp's* escort of six destroyers and launch the attack.

Three of the four torpedoes hit the vessel, two striking deep in the port side while the third caused extensive damage at the waterline. Contents of aviation fuel lines ruptured by the first two hits were ignited by the third torpedo, resulting in violent explosions rocking the ship. Water mains necessary for fire suppression had also been ruptured rendering fire fighting equipment inoperable. As a result, the fires spread unchecked throughout the vessel and the order was soon given to abandon ship.

Following evacuation of the surviving crew, the destroyer USS *Lans-downe* was ordered to deliver the *coup de grace*. Four torpedoes were launched and the USS *Wasp*, with a number of her dead crewmen still on board, sank to the bottom of the Pacific at 9pm on September 15, 1942.

But the *Wasp* and her crew did not constitute the only American involvement in the Spitfire transfer to Malta. As previously noted, the ATA has never received the recognition it so richly deserves and its brief 5½ year history is still being ignored even today. Also as previously noted, all members of the group were volunteers. Some 3,550 men and women of 28 nationalities served in the ATA. This number included over 1,100 pilots and flight engineers, of which more than 180 were American citizens and included 21 women. A total of 173 of its flying personnel were killed during the ATA's existence. At least twenty-six of those killed, including one woman, were American.

Commander James McGuinness's account, written in 1945, lists the names and ranks (at the time of the Spitfire deliveries) of the twenty four

No.4 Ferry Pool pilots involved in the transfer of the Spitfires into Abbotsinch and/or Renfrew They are as follows:

Senior Commander (S/C) Maitland W.S. Boucher, Flight Captains (F/Cs) Margaret Fairweather and Alexander Hartman Chase, Stanley Thomas Lowe, Hugh Charles Bergel, Edwin Theodore Heering and Ralph H. Henderson. First Officers (F/Os) Nathan S. Kohn, Nicholas Gibbs Pickard, Wilbur Washington Acton, Frank Rosenburg, Edmond Thornton Jarrett, Alexander Hamilton Wilson, Victor John Pieper, Ralph Gilson Jacobson, Jack Grover Durham, Derek Arthur Revers Cripps, Ernst Carl Ewing, Ernest Arthur David Kempster, Desmond Roy Huxley, James Smith Halliday, Ian Hunter Stewart, Phillip Lambert Gibbs and William Bryan Shaw.

Eleven of the pilots involved were American citizens.

The transfer of Spitfires to Malta by the USS *Wasp* has been cited as the first large-scale act of cooperation between American and British forces during the Second World War. The 24 ATA pilots listed, although seldom if ever included along with that claim, were also major participants in the two transfers which were instrumental in saving Malta. Of those 24 pilots listed, Wilbur Washington Acton, Margaret Fairweather and Ernest Arthur David Kempster were later killed in ATA service. Douglas Keith Fairweather, also a Flight Captain in the ATA, was killed just a few short months after the death of his wife Margaret in April 1944. Edwin T. Heering, Vice-Commodore of the ATA Association, lives in California and is responsible for the membership in North and South America. Recently, he reported that McGuinnes's claim of his ferrying 13 Spitfires during the transfer may have been in error as he logged only 11, but he conceded "perhaps at the end of a hard day I failed to log the other two".

McGuinnes's claim that 52 Spitfires were transported to the Mediterranean by *Wasp* during its second delivery contradicts other sources, who put the number at 50 aircraft. Perhaps the two "extras" he credited to F/C E.E. Heering account for the discrepancy.[2]

From 1940 to 1943, the tiny island of Malta and its people were subjected to continuous air attacks perhaps more terrifying and devastating (certainly in longevity) than any other Allied or Axis targets during the Second World War. Cut off from the outside world, the Maltese people were trapped and at the mercy of the Luftwaffe which was determined to capture the island that eventually earned itself the title "The Unsinkable Aircraft Carrier". Britain was quite aware of the efforts expended by the Maltese and sought to recognize their endeavours. On April 15, 1942, as the USS *Wasp* was sailing somewhere between Glasgow and Gibraltar on its first Spitfire delivery to Malta, Britain awarded the George Cross to the Maltese people for their courage and sacrifice in defending the island which played such a major part in the outcome of the war both in North Africa and in the Mediterranean.

USS *Wasp*

---

[2] EDITORS NOTE: As one of the infantrymen on the island at that time whose task it was to see the aircraft safely landed and parked in pens I feel that along with the arrival of the 'Pedestal' convoy those Spitfires were vital to winning the battle of the Mediterranean. They certainly boosted our morale!

19. WARTIME LIFE AT HAL-FAR

Nat Gold – 830 Squadron, Fleet Air Arm

I arrived at Hal-Far, Malta on 10th January 1941 to join 830 Fleet Air Arm Swordfish Squadron and take up my duties as a Telegraphist Air Gunner (T.A.G.). Strange as it may seem the squadron was the front line defence of the island. We carried out torpedo attacks on enemy convoys as well as dive-bombing over Sicily and North Africa; we also laid mines. The squadron was successful during the period from May to November 1941, sinking 110,000 tons of enemy shipping and damaging a further 130,000 tons during the same period. Some of our old Swordfish – affectionately known as 'stringbags' – were built in 1936 and had no blind flying gear or torpedo sights.

Fairey Swordfish aircraft: 830 & 828 Squadrons of the Fleet Air Arm used these out of date biplanes, known as 'Stringbags', to great effect from Hal-Far airfield in night torpedo attacks, sinking 17 of Rommel's much-needed supply ships.

After I had been on the island for six months orders were given that operational tours of all FAA and RAF air crews would be nine months on the island. When I reached the magical nine it was further reduced to six months. I therefore assumed I would be on immediate draft, but no such luck; due to lack of experienced crews I had to soldier on for twelve months. My last two months were very hectic, I never had a proper nights sleep, only cat naps, for example, after flying for several hours during the night, landing around about 7am, being debriefed, a hurried wash and shave, a quick breakfast, then turn to at 8am to service our aircraft and finally stood down at noon.

Nuisance raids prevented us getting on with our work during the morning and again in the afternoon more nuisance raids prevented sleep. Then a similar procedure the following night and day and so it went on. Our accommodation was basic; we had RAF beds with hard three hard 'biscuits' instead of a mattress. We were under RAF victualling, three meals a day against the Navy's four. For lunch I did not think it possible to disguise McConnachie's tinned stew in so many ways; another horrible meal was made from very fat tinned sausages. Our last meal of the day was at around 4.30pm – a typical meal would consist of lettuce, tomato, a spoonful of tinned salmon, a triangle of cream cheese, bread and margarine, with sometimes a wedge of melon or a slice of fruit cake. We also were given a bar of plain chocolate wrapped in a plain white wrapper. Eating this kept one going for many, many, hours.

The Naval Ratings complained about the number of meals until finally the powers that be relented and at 6.30pm we would have soup and bread; the RAF boys also enjoyed this small extra. Often we topped up our eating by having a fried egg sandwich in the NAAFI.

During the quiet periods we were fascinated by lizards running in and out of the dry stone walls; put a finger on their tail and they would shed it to make a hurried get away. Often we would stop a local girl passing by our section on the edge of the drome carrying a large basket of wild grapes; she would sell us a huge bunch for tuppence.

Many air raid alerts were false alarms and we were instructed only to take shelter after the firing of a smoke flare. Often this happened when the first screaming bomb was already on its way down. The screaming put a lot of fear into one, especially when close by, our squadron retaliated by clipping four screamers on each bomb fin. This gave us a lot of satisfaction when we went on a bombing raid. Sometimes we threw overboard empty beer bottles with a heavy stone tied to the neck; this screamed its way down, ending up with broken glass.

Jerry was very methodical; he had a set bombing routine and kept repeating it, for example, on large bombing raids he would bomb Grand Harbour, then Luqa, then Hal Far and finally Tal Kali in that order. During the air raids we either went out into the surrounding fields or down past the old Monastery on the edge of the drome to the cliffs where there were small caves to shelter in and a sheer drop of 250 feet down to very deep water.

On Wednesday 5th March 1941 the sirens sounded and the word went round that 100-plus enemy aircraft were coming in. As Luqa had been bombed last we knew it must be Hal Far's turn. Being aircrew we had no action station. In the past it had been suggested we took our Lewis or Vickers machine gun with a pan of 100 rounds of ammunition into the fields, prop it on a wall and hope for the best. It was very cumbersome and heavy to carry, making it impossible to get into position to fire upwards while holding it steady, so we soon put a stop to that.

With this particular lot approaching we evacuated into the surrounding fields to take cover in a redundant goat shelter, not very high, impossible to stand up in, but strongly built of stone. About a dozen of us stood outside and watched the aircraft coming. The first wave of Stukas went into their frightening dive and in a cloud of dust we were in the goat shelter before the first bombs came screaming down. The noise seemed to go on forever. One Stuka must have hung around up there for a while before its crew spotted us, because the scream of its bombs sounded right over the shelter. We were lying flat on the floor, almost digging in to it, when finally the bombs exploded about 10 yards away. Because the island is composed of rock and very little soil it created a greater blast effect, the explosions nearly bursting our eardrums, rocking the shelter, blowing dust and grit into our eyes and making us cough. The blast lifted me on top of an RAF LAC laying next to me; he screamed, thinking he had been hit. I had no recollection of being lifted. When the bombing ceased we plucked up courage to venture outside, only to scramble back in again as an ME109 had seen us and came in very low down the valley, firing his guns. Bullets could be heard hitting the walls and ricocheting off the roof. With our hearts racing it was a little while before we ventured outside again. When we did we went over to an Army machine gun post. They had just received a message saying that another plot of over 100 were on their way, so back we went to our goat shelter and waited for the nightmare, but fortunately this time we did not have such a close encounter. When finally it seemed to be all over we again checked with the Army post to ascertain if any more plots were on the way, there weren't, so we made our way back to the drome and hurriedly passed an unexploded bomb. We heard that 18 enemy aircraft had been shot down.

Before the raid started a local Maltese had come on his regular visit with his mule and cart to collect pigswill from the galley. On our return we came upon this poor creature, which had remained there obediently throughout all that terrible bombing. It had a large shrapnel wound in its side and was bleeding badly. One of our pilots asked us to unhitch the cart. He drew his revolver and fired one shot. The mule just shook his head. It was sickening to watch. Another was shot fired and this time the mule fell on its side, rolled on its back, kicked its legs and fell back on its side in peace. We had tears in our eyes for such a brave animal.

Returning to our billets we found utter chaos; large holes in the external walls, windows blown in, debris everywhere, we just did not know where to start clearing up. Later that day we were evacuated to Zurrieq and our first night there was an experience: sleeping on the floor with the odd rat and mouse running about and forever removing and killing fleas. During our stay at Zurrleq my roommate was shot down and interned in Tunisia.

On one particular night I had been the only T.A.G flying and on being driven back to Zurrieq, tired with no sleep after flying many hours, before going to my billet I listened to a lone German plane overhead and had a feeling he was about to off load his bombs, so I waited a while. It wasn't long before I was proved right.

The scream started and I took off to a new shelter being excavated not far away. I did not normally like going down the civilian shelters particularly in Valletta, as they would normally be crowded and very warm with everybody rattling beads and chanting the 'Rosary'. I felt like an intruder, but worst of all was the smell of garlic wafting up from the entrance, I hated the stuff, it made me want to retch. I must have beaten all race records and shot into the entrance, stumbling down the stairs in the darkness just as the bombs exploded nearby, followed by a loud, blood-curdling scream; at the same time I received a hard blow to the side of my head making me see stars. I must have been knocked out for a few seconds; when I came to I was on the floor coughing with the dust that had been blown in and could hear a woman crying and a man's voice. I scrambled up and now became accustomed to the darkness. The shelter had unfinished steps and the whole area wasn't much more than a small cavern. I noted the other occupants: a tall, well-built Maltese gentleman and his very expectant wife. I wondered why she hadn't given birth there and then; the screaming noise of the bombs and me making an unexpected fast entry must have frightened the life out of her. It was her handbag which had struck me so forcibly. We all made our apologies and I made my way back to my billet where I passed out with utter exhaustion into a deep sleep.

Next day a very strong rumour went around that during the night Jerry had dropped bars of chocolate impregnated with bacteria. I thought about this and realised the implications, but fortunately it was only a rumour.

After concentrated bombing raids on the drome it was normal for all hands to turn to, form a line across the drome and slowly walk down, picking up shrapnel fragments and sometimes helping to fill bomb craters.

It used to amaze me watching the Hurricanes take off – when they scrambled they took off in a very tight bunch, probably ten at a time. How the pilots in the rear aircraft could see one another through the dust they threw up I shall never know.

The Swordfish aircraft of 830 Squadron flew at night. When ready for take off we taxied to the beginning of a single line of dim flarepath lights which were flashed on for a while then switched off. Often Jerry waited overhead to drop anti-personnel bombs. The pilot had to memorise the flare path position then let the Swordfish roll into the darkness, inevitably struggling to take off, as we could only take off down-drome regardless of which way the wind blew, often carrying a crew of two, a full overload petrol tank in the Observer's cockpit and either bombs, torpedoes or magnetic mine, the total weight being considerable. Nevertheless, with the odd exception we managed to just clear the stone wall at the end of the drome, make our rendezvous around Fifla rock and then form into a tight "V" formation to set off on our operation. Some operations entailed over six hours flying in the old 'stringbags' and we often landed in the dark, trusting to luck that there were no new bomb craters.

Air crews had regular visits from Padres and very frequently we were handed a chit headed, 'This is not a will', requiring names and addresses of next of kin.

Three months after being evacuated to Zurrieq we returned to Hal Far on Tuesday 10th June 1941. Still no windows, the wind blew through gaping holes, and no lights. We spent evenings in the canteen or went to watch a film in the camp cinema. Sometimes in the afternoons we went swimming in the clear waters of Kalafrana Bay or played football or cricket, but the ground was not really suitable for these activities due to its rockiness. On Monday 7th July the whole camp was entertained by a concert party called the "Whizzbangs" – a group who had been in Malta before the Italians declared war and were subsequently stranded with no possibility of leaving the island. The group also entertained individually in the 'Gut', the principle character being a transvestite called 'Sugar' who was normally heavily made up and wearing a long white evening dress. He packed a mean punch if anybody upset him!

There would be great excitement if an RAF flying boat landed at Kalafrana because it heralded the arrival of mail. When we were permitted to write home it was always sprung on us – one letter, one page of air mail to be ready for censoring in 30 minutes. It was surprising how one's mind went blank under such circumstances; we were not permitted to mention anything about our work, so what else was there to say except 'I went into Valetta one evening to the cinema and then had a drink down the 'Gut" or something similarly dull?

We generally flew when the moon was up and on being stood down the doctor made we TAGs go to a rest camp at Ghain Tuffeha for four days, where we drank and swam in the sea.

At one period on the island a strong rumour became rampant that the German Commander Kesselring had begun massing gliders and gas cylinders on Sicily in preparation for the invasion of Malta. The TAGs underwent a week's intensive instruction by Army Sergeants on bayonet fighting and unarmed combat until we became sick and tired of yelling 'lunge-twist-withdraw'. On one occasion the alert had been sounded and as usual the white smoke signal fired at the very last moment. We TAGs heard the first bomb commence its bloodcurdling scream as we were doing our familiar charge across the tarmac, and headed straight for the shelter whilst the Sergeant yelled his head off for us to come back. He only just managed to escape injury by diving behind a stone wall; he didn't have our experience of such occurrences.

Both sides had their spies and fifth column. On one operation I participated in, an armed reconnaissance around the west coast of Sicily (we were carrying torpedoes in the hope of finding stray enemy shipping) we made our way round Palermo Harbour but saw nothing of interest. We flew back diagonally across Sicily in full moonlight and here and there a naked light could be seen flashing upwards.

On another occasion I had been instructed to fly in one of two Swordfish at night around and over Malta to test a new radio frequency. Not long after commencing our exercise we received a coded signal that an air raid was imminent and to take up a position East of Malta. We had a grand bird's eye view of a night attack, searchlights desperately trying to find the quarry and ack-ack and Bofors tracers. I felt quite smug but noted the odd naked light flashing upwards in the vicinity of Valletta and Sliema.

830 Squadron occasionally became involved in picking up British spies or 'bowler hat boys' as we affectionately called them, from North Africa; unfortunately we lost an aircraft on one of these operations when it got stuck in mud – the crew were interned in Tunisia.

A Heinkel 115 on floats kept at Kalfrana often took a 'bowler hat boy' to Sicily; they also had other means of transport. These British spies were marvellous and it wasn't uncommon during a briefing of a forthcoming operation that we learnt they had sent information through stating the names of ships, what they were carrying, where they were sailing from, the time of sailing, where they were destined for, and what the escort would be. They must have been running the harbours! With this information our RAF Wellingtons would be despatched to shadow the convoy and we could follow later to deliver our attack.

830 Squadron invariably armed up during the afternoon for the forthcoming night's operation but in the early evening Jerry would come over

to bomb our aircraft and put them out of action. It became more than a coincidence, but fortunately one of our ground crew had noted a goatherd sitting at the perimeter of the drome on all these occasions. He reported his observations and the Shepherd was duly arrested. The bombing ceased but nevertheless we changed the time of arming-up to early evening.

At one stage we were desperately short of torpedoes and the ack-ack gunners short of shells. Our Maltese armourers found some First World War torpedoes down at Grand Harbour which were adapted and used with fatal results; on hitting the water they just went round in circles. We were very vulnerable but fortunately Jerry did not know about this.

I finally left Malta on 25th January 1942 on HMS *Glengyle* – a little 'bomb happy' but overjoyed to be going home. We were being escorted to Alexandria by the remains of the Eastern Mediterranean Fleet, taking 2½ days of misery with constant attacks by the enemy. To get to Malta I had travelled round the Cape and I returned home the same way.

20. THE LONG JOURNEY HOME

Mrs A.B. Majoribanks Egerton

10th AUGUST 1942: The great day had arrived, we were up early to do our last packing and Anne was full of excitement, she was 6½ now and as energetic as most children of her age, in spite of a restricted diet for the past 8 months. Personal kit was limited to 50lbs per adult and 25 lbs per child, luggage was weighed and re-weighed and at last all was done.

My ex-cook, Micallef, came to help me close the quarters. He was a Gunner in the Royal Malta Artillery and had to leave that day but he insisted that he help me. Tears streamed down his face, all very awkward for me, but in spite of his tears he put in an amazing amount of work.

The morning was not without incident for a tough air battle was fought over the house when some Spitfires took on a bunch of ME109s. After some brilliant shooting two of the enemy were winged and fell in the camp area close by. We had been watching from the garden and then went back to the housework. Very childish to be so thrilled at our 2000th alert.

When all was packed we sat down to boiled cabbage, shared the 10oz bread ration and then bade Micallef farewell. A torrent of tears descended once more and we left, waving until he was lost to view at the bend of the road. Anne was not at all upset at the emotional scene; happily she was too young to realise what she had lived through for the last three years.

My husband returned during the afternoon and we took a last look at our quarters. The three dogs had gone to friends, also the canaries, all was quiet and said. Tea time came and we went to friends next door for a cup of tea. Conversation was difficult for we felt leaving very much.

At six o'clock we were up at the Guard Room ready to "embus". A crowd of friends were gathered to see us off, more families joined us, further goodbyes, then we got into the bus. Children climbed onto the seats, luggage was put in the truck, the driver got the signal to start, and we were off! A cheer went up, hands waved, we tried to return the cheers but there was an odd silence, and as we turned the corner I looked back for the last time to the camp and our quarters. Phil, my husband, looked ahead and was silent. Anne was busy with Charlie her Teddy Bear.

On sped the bus through Sliema with the inhabitants sitting at their doors, called and cheered, and one small grubby urchin waved a faded Union jack. Anne was pressing Charlie's nose against the window so that he could see things. Yes, Charlie was going to see things alright!

Eventually we came to Luqa airfield, target for endless enemy attacks. We got out of the bus and awaited orders. There was a lot to look at whilst we waited, planes being serviced ready for that night's sorties, stone pens being repaired and other bus loads of people arriving for the fly out.

We were then weighed; Anne stepped on with a hand case and Charlie, then Phil and myself. I peered at the indicator and could hardly believe that the day had come when, wearing a fur coat and carrying a case, I would weigh just seven stone. Phil registered 10 instead of his normal 12½. We certainly had been pulling in our belts pretty tightly for the last eight months.

The weighing was hardly over before an alert sounded, a very horrid moment. We moved off behind a wall and awaited results. After what seemed ages the wailing of the all clear reassured us, so back we went to the bus to be driven to the plane.

The order came to board the plane at 9pm. It was a Douglas Dakota, which seemed immense as it appeared over us like a giant. Luggage was stowed in first, then mothers with babies, more mothers and then the men. Last came the crew and the doors were closed. The captain spoke to us; we were told that there were no parachutes, that there was to be no smoking, and that the blackout was not to be touched, then he scrambled forward and the rest of the crew took their places.

The engines started up and all was darkness save for a small light over the navigator's table. There were very few seats, the plane being a troop carrier, so most of us sat on the floor, a very uncomfortable place, especially when the plane made or lost height.

Our family sat in the tail of the plane, quite near the navigator. For a time Anne sat on my lap watching him, then she fell asleep and I laid her on a couple of suitcases. Silence fell on the travellers. I started to count how many there were of us and found that with the crew we were a party of fifty. Phil had brought a bottle of Haig with him and we each had a good nip; our friends George and Charles Edwards joined us. So the night passed and I tried not to think of what would happen if the plane was attacked. I should have hated to use a parachute, but the idea of there being none was equally bad. On we sped, no one bar the crew having any idea where we were heading until at 3am the navigator said, "We are over Egypt." So that's where we were.

People began to shift and complain of stiffness and there were vague sounds of retching; a curt remark from the navigator indicated to the sufferers that 'the toilets are aft'. A torch was shone in our direction and we realised that we had sat ourselves down by that door. Soon the victims of air sickness came our way. Only by sheer will power I did not follow suit.

"We shall be landing soon," remarked the chief pilot as he came aft to speak to the navigator. We were trilled at the idea of being released from our darkness.

EGYPT, 11th AUGUST 1942: A lurch and everyone slid forward amongst the luggage. Anne woke up. Another terrific jerk and we had landed. Doors opened, voices murmured. We peered out but all was dark save for a few ground flares. RAF men stood by our plane and helped the cramp-ridden passengers down the ladders. I glanced at my watch; it was 4am, so we had been flying for seven hours. Down we got, Anne shouted: "Sand Mummy! Lots of it!" She was right; we were in the desert. She and the other children hinted at spades and buckets but such ideas were firmly quashed by exhausted mothers.

We were directed to some trucks and driven off to the RAF Mess for breakfast. What a wonderful reception we had and what hospitality given! We were ushered into the mess and asked if we would like a drink. Most voted for tea, but I said beer, yes, iced beer, even though it was only just after 4am! I had my beer amidst cheers from some RAF officers. Breakfast was then announced. We trooped off, and there, set on long tables, was a wonderful sight: pots of tea, jugs of milk, bowls of sugar, heaped plates of bread … and then appeared bacon and eggs. Anne was awestruck as she sat at the table. She looked at me and asked, "Can I have it? Is it meant to eat?" What a pathetic remark to hear from a child, and more especially from ones own child. On being assured that it was all to be eaten she said no more and just ate. Charlie was propped on her lap with his chin on the table and he too seemed amazed at the amount of food and his boot-button eyes twinkled with glee.

After eating our fill we went off for a wash-and-brush-up – a much-needed thing. Anne was full of excitement and resented being made to wash and as soon as it was all over she rushed into the sand and caught the eye of a senior officer. She soon had him helping her make a castle. I came up to him. He smiled and said that he had a daughter her age at home and a sudden sadness came into his voice when he said he had not seen her for over a year.

Later came the call that the trucks were ready. I collected Anne and Phil and we went to the truck that was to take us to Cairo. The men went in one truck and the families in another and amidst a waving of hands and many goodbyes we drew out of camp. A thirty-mile drive lay before us and the time was not yet 7 o'clock. The truck proved to be most uncomfortable: the hard wooden seats had no give in them when we bounced up and down or shot from side to side as the driver swerved to avoid camels and donkeys going our way to Cairo. The children gazed at the camels and could hardly believe their eyes. Charlie was held over the tail board to get a better view and gazed at them in bland astonishment.

Gradually we left the villages behind as we entered the city of Cairo. Traffic whirled about, despatch riders swooped past, our driver slowed down and our much-shaken insides felt a little calmer. Soon we drew up at the once-fashionable Shermiramis Hotel, now a British HQ and bustling with life and importance. The leading truck was a short distance ahead and the occupants had got out, but we were directed to "sit still", so there we sat and at once became a peepshow for the natives of Cairo.

An hour passed and by this time the children were restless. Babies wailed and over us all was the heat of Cairo in August. Someone produced a Thermos and made her baby's bottle; the less fortunate ones realised they couldn't get a Thermos till they were allowed to go shopping again.

Then, to our immense relief, a British Sergeant appeared, carrying a large tray of buns and cups of tea. We greeted him with cries of joy. He took a look at us, quickly appreciated our number and started handing out refreshments. "Here you are girls! Nothing like a cup of tea!"

We murmured our thanks. Then more troops arrived and piled us with questions as to how things were in Malta. From all they said we appeared to be considered heroines. We blushed.

"More buns! Guess you have not seen buns or cakes for months?"

The audience whistled through their teeth, hands delved into pockets and shyly owners handed up sweets.

"Come on mothers, let the poor little b****s have them".

The adjective gave no offence; we were all used to the casual way it was used in service life.

Phil soon appeared and there was a rustle of saluting from our good friends. I was told to get down, bring Anne and go with him to HQ to see about accommodation for the families. I stiffly walked into the building, which was a hive of activity. We were ushered into a lift and deposited at the Welfare Officer's Office. He asked for details concerning our numbers; I managed to answer correctly, notes were taken and then we descended again to the truck. I got in. Phil sat by the driver and we started on our way to billet families at various hotels. By noon the job was done. The heat by now was intense and I grew hotter and hotter in my thick coat and skirt. I had thought it best to wear this in view of arriving in England in early autumn. All heavy kit had to go by sea and no one could say when or if it would ever arrive (it did arrive six months later).

We had been allotted a room at the famous Continental Hotel and I was filled with shame at my weird appearance. How could I face the fashionable crowd? Phil assured me that no one would bother to look at us and even if they did, what did it matter? His kindly-meant words did little to ease my feminine mind.

The truck drew up at the pavement's edge outside the hotel and my heart sank. On the terrace sat the fashionable noontide drinkers and to gain entrance we should have to pass between the crowded tables. Ordeal by bombs was nothing to this! We made our way up the steps and I took a quick look at the drinkers. I saw 'female soldiers', quite a new thing to me, for on our island such womenfolk had not been seen.

"ATS." Phil whispered. I looked again and envied them their neat uniforms, wonderfully dressed hair, red nails, polished shoes and their male escorts, equally well groomed. Our bedraggled party was hardly in keeping with such company.

A revolving door confronted us, we were safe. The receptionist looked at us and we returned the compliment. Phil handed him the official letter, he read it, stroked an imaginary beard, took down a key from the board, waved a fat white hand and indicated the lift. The small Egyptian lift attendant beamed at us. Anne stared at him. We all got into the lift and in a few breathtaking seconds were at the 7th floor.

A charming Swiss chambermaid welcomed us and showed us to a pleasantly large room with a bathroom leading out of it, a veritable haven after the past exhausting 18 hours of travel.

"The little one is tired; she needs a sleep I think?"

I agreed it would certainly be a good thing but that she would need lunch first. Yes, that could be arranged, so after a quick tidy-up I took Anne down to the dining room. A knot of waiters gathered round. The head waiter was consulted and then a table was indicated.

"Would Madame sit here?" Madame would have been more than glad to lie on the floor, so it mattered but little to her which table she had. Anne was full of chat and told the waiter that she had flown from Malta. The effect was electric. He called in rapid French to the others and they hurried over. There was a murmur of "bombs", "Malta", "Mon Dieu" and "pauvre petite". I felt that from now on there must be no more mention of Malta if we were to have any peace. I told Anne this and she seemed rather sorry to have her big story terminated. After lunch she was bathed and put to bed and was soon fast asleep. Phil and I cleaned ourselves up and went down to lunch and a much-needed drink.

I think that I shall never forget that lunch; it was like a dream and yet one knew that it was not a dream. Some 24 hours previously we had been in Malta, dining on cabbage and very little besides, and now we had a baffling choice of dishes. Life seemed as unreal as the cinema; if one found oneself on a siege-stricken island one moment and in a well-appointed hotel the next, why worry?

After lunch we took Anne to see the shops, a thrill for us all to see full shops with things to buy. Whilst gazing in a food shop and wondering at the sight we were awakened from our dreams by a small voice.

"Daddy! Look at those Spitfires, right up there so high". Anne pointed up into an azure sky where five hawks were wheeling around. "Don't you see them?" her voice a little impatient at the grown-ups' apparent failure to recognise aircraft. We laughed and told her that they were birds, not planes. She seemed dubious, but accepted the fact and engrossed herself in a nearby toyshop. Poor Anne, to her young mind things circling high in the sky could have but one meaning; Spitfires circling ready for an attack on enemy bombers. For the last two years she had only known things like that, so to be told they were hawks was a trifle hand to accept. A toy was seen, admired and bought at the toyshop and Spitfires and hawks were forgotten in the thrill of owning a friendly clockwork monkey that 'really walked by himself'.

For the next three grilling weeks we remained in Cairo, daily awaiting orders to proceed on our way. Visits were paid to the Zoo, the Pyramids and the Gezira Club. It was nice to be back in Cairo, where we had been so happy seven years previously and where Anne had made her debut, but in spite of all the pleasantness we had no real wish to be detained any longer.

On September 2nd we were warned to be ready to leave early next day to go by sea. I was filled with presentiment that we should be torpedoed. No good thinking about it, but all the same I dreaded such a happening. I knew that I could not swim and recalled the stories I had heard about ships sinking and the frantic struggles of the drowning. I suppose we all have our personal fears and mine had always been of drowning, so for me the news that we were soon to sail for England filled me with dread.

We were up early on the morning of 3rd September and the hotel hall staff saw us off at the grim hour of 6am. Luggage was stuffed into a taxi, then ourselves and off we went to the main station. We waited an hour on the platform until other families joined us, more luggage was heaped around, children of all ages were dumped down, tempers wore thin and then, to everyone's relief, the train came in.

It did not take us long to climb in and settle down. Soon after 7 o'clock we rolled out of Cairo and were heading for Tewfik. For five hours we sat in the carriage, the heat was intense. Anne got restless, new games had to be invented, the train appeared to stop at all stations and the driver descended to greet long lost relatives.

At length we arrived at Tewfik. The noonday sun was beating down, the heat was terrific. Soon the platform was covered with harassed parents, wailing children and a melee of luggage. An officer appeared with a large list in his hand and read out: "Families to Camp X, husbands and other men to camp Z, trucks will be ready in a few minutes". At this announce-ment there was a babble of voices and a wild digging in cases to sort out washing and night tackle. No notice had been given about this segregation nor had it been hinted at, so wives had packed their husband's things in the family case. My husband and I felt rather superior as our personal effects were not packed in the same case, so we stood around while those less fortunate had to do a swift unpack on the platform.

Soon all was in order and we were getting aboard the trucks. The men went off first and there was much waving and shouting of last messages. We soon got to our camp, known locally as the 'birdcage', a barbed wired fence ran round and smart sentries guarded the gates. Three families to each tent seemed to be the usual allotment; I was lucky to have only one adult and one small child in my tent. They were very friendly and later I was to get to know her better and enjoy her friendship in London.

Lunch was served in the dining hall, a stifling place with a corrugated roof. We sat at trestle tables and were served by Italian prisoners of war. Our lunch was hardly suitable for the grilling weather, Irish Stew of a very greasy nature, this being followed by a queer-tasting trifle. One could not be particular, so we ate what we could and then escaped to our tents.

We rested until teatime, thankful for the shade and quiet. The children fell asleep and the adults relaxed. I was in that happy state betwixt asleep and waking when a voice aroused me.

"No. 10. You're wanted at the Commandant's Office, I'll show you".

I looked up. An Italian POW stood grinning at the tent door. I hurried into shoes, combed my hair and followed him over to the office. There stood Phil. He had come over from his camp to see how I was and to suggest that I came out to supper at the YMCA hut.

It seemed a good idea to me and I returned to my tent. That evening we met as planned. The large gate was swung open by the sentry, who re-minded me that I must be in by 11pm. We had a very happy time at the hut and laid plans for meeting next day at the ship; the time sped by and I found myself being challenged and then let in by the sentry. I waved to Phil as he peered through the wire fence, called 'goodnight' and then made my way to the tent. Luckily I found the right one and before long I was in bed. Anne was sound asleep and all was deadly quiet save for the distant barking of a dog. I snuggled down and must have fallen asleep in no time.

The sounds of reveille aroused me. I looked at my watch; it appeared to be 5am, dawn was breaking. Dressing and washing was coped with and then to breakfast at 6am. The Italian prisoners were still grinning.

"Good morning Missus. You take tea?" Our waiter hustled off with the order and soon returned. I should like to think that he got back to Italy when the war was over, for he seemed a very harmless type and probably had been conscripted. I bade him farewell and thanked him as we left the dining hall. He seemed very touched at this and bowed. Maybe I was taken in by his acting, maybe not.

By 7 o'clock we were all in our trucks ready for the drive to Suez. A pretty frightful road bounced us around and the hard seats of the truck were distinctly painful. At last we came to Suez; a very dirty spot. One could well realise why most people went "East of Suez". The docks were very busy and as we lined up by our trucks we had plenty of time to observe what was going on. There were five huge ships lying in the tide-way, all uniform battle grey, but one could see that they were liners in service dress; numerous small craft darted around like agitated ants.

Embarkation tickets were issued. There were no porters to help with the luggage, so we managed for ourselves. I moved up the gangway to the ferry carrying two suitcases, a bag and someone's baby. Anne went ahead carrying Charlie and her case. Soon we were under way and heading for one of the liners; the sea was choppy and several faces took on an olive hue. Before long we had drawn alongside the ship and I saw, painted out, the name *Oransay*. She towered above us, very large and very grey.

We were marshalled up the gangway of the *Oransay*, no easy task with my assorted burden. I made the steep gradient but then dropped my handbag and a mirror fell to the deck and smashed. Remembering the superstition of a broken mirror and on a Friday too, I hurriedly gathered the bits together into my handbag and made my way to where Phil had now come to join us. We had a nice cabin, small but the great thing was that we were together. I told him about the mirror and he wrapped the bits in paper and at a convenient time dropped it out of the porthole. Some hours later we sailed; the beginning of an adventure by sea. I remembered the broken mirror, remembered it was Friday and also that there were five persons aboard; surely we must have bad luck before long. What about the presentiment coming true?

We passed down the Gulf of Suez and entered the Red Sea. The heat was intense and no cool air at night, for all the portholes were shut and strictly blacked out, so we sweated hour after hour as the Prime Minister had so truly said. It was the War Effort with a vengeance. Again I was to remember it as I strove to do the family wash in a room resembling a heated Turkish Bath, ironing drill in a room well over 100°F is no joke. Yes, we girls "toiled and sweated" all right, and near to tears too.

Our first stop was Aden. No one was allowed ashore so we hung over the rails in the time-honoured way, watching new arrivals come aboard. RAF personnel came up the side, bags of mail were swung on and off, and before long we were on our way again. The aggressive heat continued all the way down the Red Sea. Social life aboard ship was very pleasant. The ship's officers were most friendly, bi-weekly dances were organised and I found that even though there might be submarines around and the deck was often at an alarming angle, the lure of the dance still held me. I had crammed an old evening dress (some 6 years old) into my Malta case and also a pair of dancing shoes, so I was ready for the ball.

Days passed quietly and nights cheerfully and we reached Durban on September 16th. It was springtime in South Africa. Masses of flowers were on sale and I lost no time in buying some. A wonderfully well-planned town Durban: spacious sidewalks, ornaments, tress and well-swept roads. I suppose the shops attracted us most with all their pre-war goods – a most wonderful sight. Everyone was allowed ashore for part of each day.

A great shock awaited us on 20th September when we were told to pack up and be ready to transfer to the *Duchess of Atholl*. In a few hours the changeover was done and goodbyes said to our kind friends on *Oransay*. Where was she going? Of course no one knew. All very secret.

The *Duchess of Atholl* was 20,000 tons and had been used as a trooper. There had been no time to clean her up and I need hardly describe the mess that awaited us. Of course there were no stewardesses and only a few stewards. Our cabin was a large pre-war double cabin, now converted to a 4-berth. No sheets on the beds and the blankets smelt of their last owners, but one could not be too particular – there was a war on.

I inspected the lavatories close by, a very revolting sight. Another woman had the same idea of an inspection, a capable Scots type. We interviewed the steward. "Not My Job". But if we liked to draw brushes, pails and Harpic, well … no one would say no. Thus armed as a sanitary squad we tackled the job, after which things looked decidedly better and we pictured rising generations being able to hang thoughtfully over the bowl's edge without being engulfed in weeks of dirt. We knew how small children of two or three years seem intrigued with the inside of sanitary-ware and would gaze like Selina into the depths.

So much for this strange task afloat; the first of many before I was to get to England. Later that day we left Durban and various rumours went round as to our next port of call. The captain spoke to us all in the large lounge. He pointed out that we were at war, that submarine attacks were probable, that lifeboat drill must be strictly observed, blackout attended to and that no rubbish was to be dropped overboard; this was vitally impor-tant as submarines tracked ships for miles by dropped refuse. In case of an emergency a siren would sound. Lifebelts were to be carried at all times. No bathroom doors etc were to be locked.

The sea was getting rougher as we went on our way. The tables grew emptier at meals. The hearty walkers decided not to do their "round the decks" walks. We as a family were luckily in the "good sailor" department but survived a pretty trying time till we got to Cape Town on the 25th. What a marvellous experience it was to see Table Mountain in the first light of dawn. The lights of the town were dying out and soon the mountain was lit by the sun's rays. Soon the whole mountain and town was ablaze with sunlight.

We spent a short time in Cape Town and then steamed out to Saldhanu Bay where we anchored for five of the longest days ever known; the most trying of the whole trip. Everyone grew bored and restless and longed to go ashore. Our release came on the 30th when we turned and went back to Cape Town. We were allowed ashore for so many hours per day and took full advantage of our good luck. The town impressed us. It was well planned with broad streets and imposing buildings and the shops were a veritable treasure trove. Spring was just coming in and I have yet to see a more wonderful sight than the lower market. Baskets seemed to spill their colours all around. We got daffodils and violets, small pineapples and bananas as well as more necessary shopping.

In the midst of all this I came down with a very sudden attack of influenza and went to bed not caring whether I survived or not. The thermometer showed 103 degrees. I viewed the cabin with double vision. Some friends of the *Oronsay* came to say goodbye before they started for home and with the usual humour of friends bade me to take my drink with more water and thus avert the double vision. I said nothing!

On October 30th we sailed. The journey had begun again and we were now on the most dangerous leg. The captain spoke to us once more and reminded us of our lifeboat drill and the necessity of carrying our belts with us at all times. Having heard him I retired to bed again, feeling very weak. On the 5th I was up all day trying to get my legs into working order. Smith the steward bade me go easily; I assured him I would.

We ran into very heavy weather directly we headed north. The ship rolled and tossed like an inebriated elephant, every timber creaked, everything that could slide in the cabin slid, few people came in for meals. As a family we survived, but had times of feeling decidedly fragile. Boat drill was a bi-daily routine and we kept a bag packed with personal papers, bits of jewellery, etc – a relic from the Malta days when I had always carried around my "escape bag".

So life went on until the morning of 10th October 1942.

At 6.30 am a terrific jarring shook the ship. I was awake and contemplating, Phil was awake and Anne asleep. I put up my hand to switch on the light but there was no response, it was still the blackout hours.

"We seem to have hit something," said Phil. I could but agree. We both knew what we suspected. "Better get up and dress."

I got out of bed and tried to dress quickly but a curious numbness seemed to bind my limbs and make my fingers like wool. Phil dressed too, we were very silent. No now we could hear a scream or two as people realised what had happened.

Doors opened and shut and then all was deadly quiet. I was at last dressed but had forgotten that most important part of female dress, my bra – and was bitterly to regret it for the next week.

A tap at the door and Smith looked in. "No need for alarm … torpedo sir. I will leave this lamp in the corridor; no electricity." Then he was gone; a master of the British art of understatement.

I had, by now, got Anne up and dressed her; no easy task as she was very sleepy and uncooperative. The word came for us to proceed to the deck. We packed what we could – a dreadful moment, having to leave all ones belongings.

"All up on deck, please." Smith flitted past and we joined the throng now moving up onto the boat decks. No panic, all very calm, very orderly, we might have been going to breakfast instead of taking to the boats. I shook with emotion and trusted that if anyone noticed it I should pass as being cold. Anne clutched Charlie as I carried her in my arms. Up we went and at last were out on the open deck. All life belts were on and adjusted.

We stood by our allotted boats awaiting orders. I found that I had left my wristwatch behind and in a selfish moment told Phil. He was given leave to go, but at his own risk. Another man went too on a similar errand. Time seemed to pass deadly slowly and I pictured the ship sinking with Phil trapped below. I gazed out to sea, huge waves rushed past, I felt sick.

"Couldn't find the watch darling, but I brought these." To my utter relief, there was Phil and in his hand lay the lipsticks I had got at Capetown. I felt like crying but just muttered "Thanks." He said the ship was all dark below and not a soul about. He had used his torch and raced along, fearing that at any moment she would be hit again.

A shudder ran through the ship. We swayed. A burst of excitement. Another torpedo? Keep calm. Whistles went. "Lower the boats".

Everything moved with precision. Our boat was swung out over the side then drawn in and held.

"First ones in, go slow, plenty of time," the steady voice of our boat's chief directed us. Anne was the first to go and she climbed into the boat assisted by a sailor. Charlie was under her arm. She went forward and sat down. I followed her, then three other women, a baby (9 months) and a six year old girl. Then came the men of the party.

The sea surged and the waves heaved. The drop from the boat deck of a 20,000-ton liner is no small way and now looked immense.

"Hold on tight Anne darling. Shut your eyes and keep still," said Phil and at that moment the boat began to slide down on the davits. I felt horribly afraid but soon the violent rocking motion occupied my senses. We were on the sea. We were safely down.

The sheer side of the *Duchess* rose steeply above us and the decks were lined by Army and RAF personnel. Wild cheers broke out as they saw us safely afloat. Our oarsmen started to pull away from the ship; no mean task on that heavy sea.

"Come on Cambridge!" "Come on Oxford!" shouted the troops. "Remember me to mother," called a lone voice. Less suitable remarks were shouted and then more and more cheers broke out as further boats drew away. Our oarsmen were having a very stiff time keeping the boat away from the ship and preventing her getting swamped by the huge waves.

Anne watched the *Duchess* with interest. "Look Charlie! See all those sailors letting down the boats?" His boot-button eyes seemed to gaze in admiration at the crews. I fancied I heard him say "Well done boys!"

Then I became appallingly sick and my reputation of being a "good sailor" rapidly faded. I cared but little what happened to me, everyone suffered to some degree and the apologies at first so noticeable, soon were absent as the sound of retching rent the air. I leant my head in the lap of a gunner officer who had indicated that he was quite agreeable to such forward behaviour. As I struggled with the waves of sickness I heard a voice say "she's going…" I thought I must surely be pretty bad if death was so near. I raised my head and Phil said, "Look… over there… she's had it".

I looked and saw the *Duchess* going down. There was an immense roar and a cascade of water as the third and last torpedo struck her well forward. She swayed and then steadied, then, on a rope just by the bows, slid several figures into a small boat.

"There goes the Old Man," said a sailor near to me. Yes! The old man had stayed till the last and was now getting away, and not a moment too soon! The *Duchess* was listing badly, smoke poured from her funnels and the ensign fluttered from her stern like a trapped bird. Then she rolled sharply onto her side and very slowly and painfully slid under the waves. The sea boiled and hissed around her and at once wreckage came to the surface. Hundreds of oranges bobbed about (part of the cargo), spars, furniture and not far off surfaced the enemy with the crew lined up on deck, the Hun submarine.

She hung around like some dark hound, we waited for the boats to be searched and feared we might get a burst of fire. The men in our boats wearing caps took them off and hid the badges, moments passed and to our relief the submarine dived and we were alone. The time was now soon after 9am. The *Duchess* had taken three hours to sink and had received three torpedoes before she died. The total number of casualties was five, all in the engine room from the first torpedo; they had died instantly.

As the morning wore on I became less sick and was able to notice things. I realised that no-one could possibly say how long it was to be before help came and I must say that the thought of slowly drifting till death released one was hardly cheering. We were about 50 souls in our boat, three children, four women and the remainder men. We sat on the narrow seat, the water up to mid-calf, owing to a leak. The sun beat down and we soon became very sunburnt, the children being the worst sufferers, but we could do nothing for them. Shifts were taken at the oars by the men with we women relegated to the stern and part of the sail erected lengthwise to give us a bit of privacy. It was behind this screen that the necessities of life were performed, a pretty tricky job balancing on a small bucket with the boat bobbing like a cork. However 'needs must' and we soon lost any sense of shame when we requested that the bucket be passed to the "Harem". We were, indeed, lucky to be in a boat and not on a raft.

So the day wore on, rations of very dry biscuits, chocolate and Horlicks milk tablets were issued – all very difficult to swallow and usually made one very sick. A small ration of water was dealt out. Some of us had salvaged oranges as they bobbed past and in spite of their salty flavour we were glad to have them for the children. I think the most pathetic sight was to see the baby of the party suffering great discomfort from lack of proper food and then it howled. Its mother tried to comfort it with bits of biscuit but the child was under a year old and could not eat food like that.

When evening came sails were hoisted and from the company of the forty other boats came the sound of that popular tune "Red Sails in the Sunset". We were far out at sea with no immediate prospect of being picked up. Darkness fell and the children were settled as well as could be arranged for the night. A last meal of chocolate biscuits was handed out, topped off with a sip of water. We had orders not to row at night for fear of losing touch with the other boats. Contact was made by flashing torches and calling out. Another woman and myself were directed to drop the sea anchor. I had never set eyes on such a thing, much less handled it. We were able to carry out the job and dropped what looked like a very large jelly bag over the stern and fix its rope to the mast. All night long the boat tossed and pitched, the air was cold and I was glad that I had been firm about wearing my fur coat when we took the boats.

At 2am a very big wave hit the boat and we thought that we had gone. Everyone called out and after gasping through a sheet of salt water we were again on even keel. I was extremely alarmed and clung to Phil, who with his usual calm outlook told me not to worry. The dawn gradually came and never had I been so glad to see the sun rise as I was that Sunday morning in mid-ocean.

The Catholic padre offered a short prayer and then tasks were allotted for the day: so many hours rowing, so many hours bailing out. The sea anchor was drawn up and once more we were on our way. Anne was full of chat and asked if we were going to England in the boat; a groan came from the oarsmen at such a prospect.

It was a very sunny day and the waves a trifle calmer, numerous Nautilus floated past, a very pretty sight, and the flying fish skimmed along, but in spite of these diverse attractions I kept wondering when we would be rescued. So on we rowed. By now it was close on 8am and there had been some talk about breakfast. Then came that staggering moment when the shout went up.

"There's smoke over there, look!"

We looked. We peered.

"Can't you see it? A thin wisp."

We looked again, afraid that we might be under the wrong impression, and then watched fascinated. To our joy it was not getting less. I think that tears were not far from me, but I could hardly give way, so I arrested them early on and gazed spellbound at the smoky trail.

Then a speck appeared in the sky from the direction of the smoke.

"Plane! Keep down, it may be an enemy!"

The speck grew bigger and bigger and soon was roaring over us as we crouched in the boat to avoid a possible burst of gunfire. It swooped over us as we looked up and saw a white star on each wing and fuselage.

It was American; we were saved.

We cheered. We stood up and waved. I tried to cheer too but no sound came. Back came the plane the pilot waving and then he was gone.

Conversation broke out, some sang, some whistled, we were souls reborn. Breakfast was eaten with zest. We had the hope of life again. The nightmare was ending.

"Mummy save him quick!" Anne's voice was shrill with alarm. I collected my wits and saw Charlie floating face down in the water at the bottom of the boat, being drawn closer and closer to the outlet valve. I scooped him up and wrung him out, a sad soggy mass with his fur clinging to his trim figure and his knitted coat shrinking visibly. He was pinned to the mast by one hand to dry and his small mother eyed him tearfully, not very amused at the grown-ups' apparent lack of good taste in laughing at such a disaster.

Boats were headed for the smoke on the horizon which came ever nearer and soon we discerned the outlines of an Armed Merchant Cruiser. It was past noon when we drew near enough to hear directions shouted through a megaphone.

"Row like hell. Keep at it!" Our rowers made no comment and bent all backs to the task of bringing the boats alongside; no easy task in such a heavy sea. One mistake and we could be crushed against the side of our rescuer. The crew hung over the side, giving us directions and advice. A rope ladder was hanging over the side and up this we had to make our way. The children went up in a basket. Anne wanted to go up the ladder but her father firmly pushed her into the basket and in a moment she was up on deck calling out to us "Come on!"

Gradually our boat emptied and then it was my turn to go up the ladder. I awaited the word "NOW!" and as our boat rose on the top of the wave I swung onto the ladder. I felt horribly sick with fear as I glanced down at the surging water but with bare swollen feet and my bag over my shoulder I started on my way up. Before I knew it I was on deck being complimented for the good time I had made in my climb.

"Come along mother and have some tea." A sailor showed me where the nectar lay. Anne ran ahead and there, sure enough, was tea and heaps of bread and butter. Amidst a buzz of voices we found out that all our boats had been picked up and that during the night we had drifted 40 miles from the *Duchess*.

So much has already been told about the kindness of the British Navy and yet I do not think that one more story will be out of place. The small babies of our party had no change of clothes, so down in the sick bay, which had been hurriedly made into a nursery were a party of burly sailors cutting up tiny vests from rolls of lint, these were then sewn and the babies bathed and dressed. Bottles were filled and applied. Yes! The Royal Navy were super-men!

The doctors worked hard to ease the pain of the sunburn and I had my legs seen to, as they were beginning to swell badly from exposure in the salt water for 30 hours. I then went below to help get the children sorted out and washed. No one had any washing things and no toothbrushes; however one can do a lot with one's hands.

The Petty Officers Mess was turned over to the women and children – a tiny and intensely hot room reached from the deck by way of a precipitous ladder. We took turns to wait and serve at meals and dripped in the heat. The male survivors were fed on deck, no plates, no spoons or forks. Phil had an empty peach tin as cup and plate and insisted on brining it home as a reminder of that grim incident of wartime.

Our rescue ship HMS *Corinthian* was a heavily-armed and carrying a crew of one hundred and yet we were taken aboard – our number being 820 – so it needs little imagination to realise how cramped we were for space. For five days we were guests aboard the *Corinthian*. We slept on deck, had no blankets or pillows, sleeping space was very crowded but no one ever complained. The decks ran with moisture after the night dews and one began to suffer from rheumatism, but this was acceptable; anything rather than being adrift in a lifeboat.

The children soon settled down to life again and mothers tried to wash clothes. Anne ran around in a large handkerchief pinned on like pants whilst I washed her cotton dress and pants. She had lost her shoes in the boat and bar her coat, dress, pants and Charlie had no worldly goods. I had a vest, cotton dress, pants and fur coat, also my escape bag.

Personal washing was carried out in mob formation amidst the crews quarters. Cloakroom accommodation was limited but met with every courtesy by the crew with profuse apologies if they appeared whilst the ladies were 'enthroned' or engrossed in washing.

The day following our rescue, services of thanksgiving were arranged by padres of all denominations. The strains of "Eternal Father" rose in strong opposition to other hymns and I doubted if it had ever been sung before with so much meaning and fervour.

On October 15th we arrived off Freetown in humid weather and a series of heavy rainstorms. The anchor was let go and a tender appeared alongside to take survivors off. We bade goodbye to our kind friends and tried to thank them for everything. There seemed misty eyes on both sides and our three cheers were not as brisk as they might have been.

We drew alongside the *Nea Hallas* and then down came the tropical rain and in a second we were all soaked to the skin. At that moment an American soldier stepped in front of me and said "Say Mom, I want to take a snap of you and the kids to send back home, kinda remind them that there's a war on." He put his cine camera to his eye and I suppose

"Back home" later received a weird picture of an Englishwoman and several children that had been recently torpedoed and then thoroughly soaked in a tropical downpour.

As we proceeded up the gangway to go aboard our new ship we must have appeared a very bedraggled lot to the many passengers leant over the side to watch our arrival. All women and children were directed to the State Drawing Room and handed over to the Relief Committee. Here we were advised to go to our cabins and then report back when changed, but had this order been carried out many of us would have had to pose as Eve without the benefit of a fig leaf! The head of the committee saw what a stupid order had been given and then and there we were issued with a change of clothing and duly departed to put ourselves in order. We then discovered that the order had been given for the men to be on one side of the ship and women and children on the other. A great cry went up from us all. This arrangement would never do. We had survived a crisis and were not prepared to face another in the shape of being segregated. I had a deputy, who waited on the Purser, who handed the matter to the Captain, who would not give a reply until the ship had sailed, so that night married families carried out their own orders and next day our petition was granted and we settled down to the home run with happy minds.

Our ship was packed with survivors from 72 other ships that had met with disaster during the last month off South Africa. Harrowing tales were told and we soon realised that our episode had been a very mild affair when compared with the sufferings from those of such ships as the *Andorra Star*". News was confirmed that the *Oransay* had gone down on October 9th and that there was little hope of there being any survivors. This was very shocking news; we could but hope that some of them had been saved.

Just before we left Freetown on the 19th the last party of survivors came abroad and those survivors were part of the crew of the *Oransay*. We went to meet them but what a dreadful shock it was to fail to recognise them.

Due to exposure from nearly two weeks in open boats they had large blisters from sunburn which covered their faces; eyes were sunken and lips so swollen that speech was difficult. Walking was an effort and we realised that we could not worry them with questions. Those who have not seen the effects of exposure in open boats cannot realise how much human beings can suffer and how dreadful it is to fail to recognise friends because of such horrors. How wonderfully fortunate we had been; we could never be too thankful. Later we learnt that our greatest friends from the *Oransay* had been picked up and were safely aboard another ship nearby.

On October 19th we left Freetown; the heat was tiring and our nerves a trifle jaded. The blackout at night was torture as one lay and sweated, knowing that the portholes would remain barred until morning. My legs had become septic and I was ordered to the sick-bay. I pleaded against going but the doctor was adamant and so I found myself in bed. I lay and worried as to what would happen if we were torpedoed? I knew that I could not get to Phil and Anne. The sick-bay was over the engine room and I knew that such a spot was a very likely target. After three worrying days I was allowed to return to my family, my legs swathed, but at least I was free, and that was all I wanted.

Various lifeboat drills were held daily. Sunday services came and went and we could hardly smother a smile when the gospel for that first Sunday was that of warning us not to lay up for ourselves treasures on earth. Alas our treasures were reposing at the bottom of the Atlantic and we need have no fear of 'corruption by moth or rust'.

The weather began to grow colder as we neared England. Most of us had only cotton dresses, a few had coats; luckily I had clung on to my fur coat and was now in a superior position. I had but one cotton dress and one undergarment to go with such a coat, but such are the vagaries of war.

On 30th October we anchored off Greenock and were able to have our first glimpse of Britain since 1938. The next day we moved off again and by evening were made fast in the docks of Glasgow. After an early supper we went ashore at 8pm. Everywhere was pitch black save for a few arc lamps skilfully shaded close to the ship. We were assembled on the quay-side and shivered in the cold night air in our inadequate garments. Orders were awaited and time passed very, very slowly. A large group of airmen close by broke into song with "Why are we waiting?" and the tune was that usually connected with "Come all ye Faithful". Soon we all joined in and for a time the quayside loafers were regaled with a new song to an old tune, then the song faded out and we became silent and bored.

It was not until 11pm that the order came to proceed, so on numbed feet we tottered off, small children crying from sheer weariness, dragged at heel. We picked our way in the near blackout to the platform. No easy task to navigate tired children over railway lines in darkness whilst coping with bundles and thinning tempers, but all was safely accomplished and we eventually came to a halt in mid-line and discovered that we were along-side a train.

"Climb up and get settled," was the order from the Military Policeman.

Now a train by a platform is one thing, but a train on an open line is another and from where we stood it seemed a sort of first cousin of the Eiffel Tower as regards height. However, orders are orders, and soon we were handing the children up, then the bundles and then, amidst giggles and exclamations, we scrambled up the high steps.

The train was unheated and dimly lit and we were warned that we would not get to London until noon next day. No food and no drink were provided. It seemed to us that this was the last straw, but it was no good complaining and so we settled down for what was to be a 12-hour journey. No seats to lie on either, we had been allotted coaches of the 4-to-a-table type; another bitter blow as it would mean sitting up all night for anyone over child size.

At midnight we slowly drew out of Glasgow and started on a most long and tiring journey to London. Sleep was out of the question and when the blinds were permitted to be raised dawn was just coming up and we all looked pretty worn out. We were cold, hungry, thirsty and extremely dirty. The sanitary conveniences were primitive with little or no water and long before we got to London the word 'pull' was a mockery. It was hard to get the children to realise that there was no breakfast and yells of disappointment rent the air. Cries of "I'm thirsty" were oft repeated and exhausted mothers gave up reasoning and let their offspring cry themselves out.

Thus the morning wore on until at noon we drew into London and hurried attempts to "get tidy" were gone through before we stepped down from the train, said our goodbyes and once more became individuals for the first time in over 11 weeks.

We headed directly for the haven marked 'BUFFET' and it was in a long glass there that I caught a glimpse of what I looked like. A grim sight met my eyes and for a moment I wondered who it was standing there. If I really looked like that I had better avoid looking-glasses in the future!

Phil and I had beer and buns and Anne lemonade and buns; Charlie viewed the room from under Anne's arm and looked slightly exhausted after all his adventures.

We phoned our relatives in Hampstead and reached there by taxi. We rang the bell, the door opened and amidst a chorus of excited voices we went in.

The trek was over. We had made it!

Major Phillip Majoribanks-Egerton (seated)
with daughter Anne and her teddy-bear Charlie.

Mrs Anne Syzmusik Nee Majoribanks-Egerton with Charlie,
who is still around after surviving so many adventures.

21. A Rookie's Tale

John Willoughby, RNVR – HMS Nubian

Much emphasis has been placed on the defence of Malta during its Siege Years of 1940-1942 in the Second World War but the island's activities were not confined to defence alone. For example; in April 1941 there were based four striking destroyers, HMS *Jervis* and HMS *Janis* (J-Class) and *Nubian* and *Mohawk* (Tribal Class) of the Royal Navy's 134th Destroyer Flotilla. In addition there was a flotilla of eight 'U' class submarines and the RAF was busy raiding Sicily and Italy whilst also attacking enemy convoys heading for North Africa.

Nubian first visited Malta late in May 1940 on her way to join the eastern fleet in Alexandria. After being bombed in the Norwegian Fiords, frozen in the Atlantic ocean and tossed about in a turbulent North Sea, the Mediterranean was like paradise: warm, smooth, sunny, no enemy activity and no tension; it was unbelievable.

Once in Alexandria the lower deck was cleared; this meant that all ratings had to assemble on the forecastle to be addressed by the captain.

"I have to tell you," he said, "that diplomatic relations between our government and the government of Italy are very bad. The first indication that Italy has declared war may well be in the form of an air attack on our ships in Alexandria. Therefore extreme vigil at all times is essential."

How unfortunate that American ship's companies were not similarly addressed at Pearl Harbour before December 7th 1941. Two weeks later in the evening of June 6th 1940 Italy declared war. The lower deck was not afraid, after all, it could not possibly be worse than Norway, and the *Nubian* could look after itself.

Tribal class destroyers were the biggest and most powerful in the whole British Navy. For surface action their main armament consisted of four gun mountings, each with two 4.7-inch guns producing a salvo of eight 4.7-inch shells. These were supplemented by a nest of four torpedoes. For defence against aircraft there was a multiple-barrelled Pom-Pom gun known as 'The Chicago Piano' and on each side of the ship were rapid fire four-gun 0.5-inch mountings. For attacks on submarines depth charges could be rolled off from the stern mechanism and also fired from port and starboard throwers.

Nubian had one weak link in the form of a 'rookie' ordinance officer artificer. This was not entirely his own fault. At the outbreak of World War II Higher National Certificates were asked to fill in a miscellaneous 20-page form before joining the forces. The rookie's HNC was in Electrical Engineering and, as the Royal Navy would not then accept Electrical Artificers for a period of less than 12 years, he had been badly channelled into the Ordinance Branch. This ludicrous situation soon changed and men similarly qualified were being offered wartime electrical commissions.

Meantime 'the rookie', as he had been called, was happy aboard. Everything was new, lots to be learned and he was on good terms with his tutor, the chief OA. He also strengthened the ship's football team.

When Italy declared war on all eastern Mediterranean naval activities, including those Malta-related, all destroyers became very active, with duties including escorting battleships, cruisers and Malta convoys, carrying out bombardments and the odd evacuation. Now, with memories dimmed, only salient points can be reported...

"The best form of defence is attack." So said Admiral Andrew Cunningham, Commander in Chief Eastern Mediterranean Fleet and, to show he was boss he engaged the Italian Fleet off Calabria on 9th July 1940, chasing it back at full speed to the safety of its own harbours, *Nubian*, leading the destroyer charge, was straddled but not hit by enemy shells, whose whirling sounds were plainly heard. Their tones were different from those bombs dropped off Norway and not pleasant. From sinking ships came survivors and the easiest way of getting them on board was by using grabbing nets (nets of rope rolled down the ship's sides amidships). Naturally left-handed, the rookie became helpful on the nets, going down on one side with a right-handed man on the other side. Up top, giving instructions, was the first lieutenant.

"There is too much swearing on board and it has to stop," said the Captain. "The first man I hear swearing will be punished."

For days nothing happened, then, up in the crows nest, the most isolated place on board, the duty lookout was being relieved.

"Its bloody well raining again," said the relief. The sound travelled down the voice pipe onto the bridge and right into the port side ear of the Captain. How unlucky can one get?

Incidentally both "port" and "left" have four letters; it is therefore easy to remember that portside is left side and starboard must be right side. It took 'you-know-who' years to find that out!

On Novmeber 14th 1940 the Commander-in-Chief struck again when Fairey Swordfish torpedo bombers from the aircraft carrier *Illustrious* attacked enemy warships in Taranto harbour. In this daring and brilliantly executed attack the enemy battleship *Cavour* was sunk and the battleships *Littorio* and *Caio Diulio* were seriously damaged.

The Fleet Air Arm Museum in Somerset provides a brochure in which visitors are invited to view this incident in World War II by means of a "unique visitor-operated push button action diorama which brings to life with flares, anti-aircraft fire and tracer, torpedo and bomb bursts, as flights of Fairey Swordfish aircraft attack the burning ships – as though the viewer was 8,000 feet over the harbour". No mention is made of the Commander (Air) Guy Willoughby who trained most of the pilots and regarded Taranto his greatest achievement. He died recently, disappointed at not having made full Admiral rank.

Acting as decoys, *Nubian* and another destroyer went into the Adriatic and sank an enemy ship going from Italy to Albania, rejoining the main fleet the following morning.

The Straits of Alranto were mined and the announcement "The ship is about to pass over a minefield, close all portholes and scuttles" frightened the life out of the Rookie. Mines were another thing he knew nothing about, while everyone else seemed to take them for granted. How did they react to varying speeds of the ships? Where were the ship's most vulnerable points? Like everything else in the Navy, the deeper he thought, the more complicated it became.

A successful Malta convoy was followed by the ship's company being given night leave and some chief and petty officers spent it at the Sergeants Mess in Army Barracks. After the bar closed the naval types slept on easy chairs and returned to their ship the following morning. When back on board one Chief Petty Officer found he did not have his false teeth and asked the next man to arrive if he had seen them.

"Yes," he was told. "There were some teeth in a chair."

"Didn't you bring them back?" he was asked.

"No Chief," came the answer. "I couldn't lift the easy chair!"

This time leaving Malta was different; instead of returning directly to Alexandria the ship was going to Gibraltar before returning to base. This meant going through the dreaded Pantelleria Straits, normally negotiated at night with minimum noise. Unfortunately engine trouble developed right in the danger zone and steam relief valves began to blow, producing so much noise the ship turned around and returned to Malta. The rookie slept through it all – the beer in Malta was strong at that time.

One night with the evacuation of Greece in progress, a boat thought to be an enemy motor torpedo boat was sighted out at sea. This was unexpected and with guns at the ready the destroyer moved in to investigate. Suddenly from the boat came a stream of abuse with Birmingham intonation and expletives strong enough to shock the devil.

"Get them aboard!" said the Captain.

Captain Mack (codename D14) working from *Jervis* was Commanding Officer of the Flotilla which included the Tribals *Nubian* and *Mohawk* and when *Jervis* was not available for sea because of maintenance or boiler cleaning etc, he and his staff transferred themselves to *Nubian*. What a damned nuisance that was! Junior officers turfed out of their cabins, ship's petty officers told what they should do and how they should do it and so on. They thought they were God's chosen few!

"Two men in the sea starboard thirty," shouted the lookout in the crow's nest. A boat was lowered and an Italian petty officer in a life jacket with an officer holding on behind were picked up. They had apparently been alone in the middle of the ocean for nine hours. First aboard was the officer who declined the use of the waiting stretcher and staggered unaided to the sick bay. Next came the petty officer, shaking and delirious, to be stretchered off for medical attention. After a recovery period he became a guest of the petty officer's mess. When back in harbour the caterer gave him a huge pack of sandwiches with a large screw-topped bottle of water. The torpedo PO, whose pet hobby was denouncing enemy personnel, gave him a packet of cigarettes and the rookie OA gave him a rosary, which excited him. He then took off a necklace with a golden pendant of the Blessed Virgin Mary, the size of a sixpenny piece, and presented it to the mess. This was not acceptable and the gunner's mate spoke to him like he spoke to his defaulters and this had the desired effect. After handshakes all round the prisoner left under guard. Why the hell were we fighting each other?

On one occasion *Nubian* was in Alexandria's dry dock undergoing minor repairs while the whole Fleet went out to sea and her ship's company enjoyed the rare privilege of walking ashore in the market streets while others ploughed the ocean. For their pleasure was the Fleet Club, which made a NAAFI beer bar seem like the Ritz, several licensed restaurants, and a sprinkling of do-goody places, usually with religious bents, where service personnel could get tea, biscuits and cakes at reduced prices. Into one such place went the rookie to be greeted by a superior young lady who welcomed her only customer by showing her teeth and pretending to be pleased. After a de-icing interval and knowing he was unlikely to get another chance like this he suggested a meeting together on the following evening, perhaps a meal in a five star hotel, a box at the theatre or a tombola session at the Fleet Club?

"Not tomorrow evening," she said. "I shall be going out with the Queen of Egypt. Now let me see … the evening after?"

"Not a chance," said the rookie. "I shall be dining with the Admiral!"

He left. No use staying in a place like that. The Queen of Egypt indeed!

The battle of Matapan took place on March 30th 1941. In the battle the Eastern Mediterranean Fleet under the command of Admiral Andrew Cunningham, flying his flag on the battleship *Warspite*, damaged the Italian battleship *Vittorio Veneto*, sunk three heavy cruisers – *Zara*, *Fiume* and *Pola* and destroyers *Vincento Gioberti* and *Maestrale*. As this battle has been well documented the following report deals only with the cruiser *Pola* from the time it was abandoned on even keel with guns still pointing fore and aft.

Nubian, whose captain later claimed any British captain abandoning a ship in a similar condition would be court marshalled, was invited to go in and finish her off. The captain positioned his ship parallel to and pointing in the same direction as the cruiser and fired a torpedo. Maybe *Pola* was bigger than *Nubian* and at night refraction can play tricks; evidently the gap between the ships was been bigger than imagined because nothing happened. After what seemed ages someone said, "Oh dear, we have missed." The torpedo officer was ranting, "I shall resign! I shall resign!" when eventually a fountain of water began rising from the cruiser's amidships. The Italian heavy cruiser *Pola*, stopped by the aircraft carrier *Formidable*'s bombers, then battered to submission by Cunningham's battleships, quietly turned over on her side and according to one torpedo man "went down like a soft fart".

The next job was to take on prisoners, men who called the Mediterranean "*Mare Nostrum*" (my sea). Exactly how many were pulled in to chants of "*mare nostrum*, you bastards, *mare nostrum*" heaven alone knows – perhaps three parts of a ship full. Prisoners in such numbers cannot be accommodated without inconvenience and on the following morning one irascible stoker was going round saying, "My towel looks as though it has been used by half the Italian fleet".

The rookie was chatting with his assistant who was on guard duty on the seaman's mess deck. Pointing at his prisoners he said, "You know chief the difference between us and them is, we mess ourselves and carry on, they mess themselves and abandon ship", or words to that effect.

In the petty officer's mess, up the companion way and through a hatch from the seaman's mess, the medical PO was upset. A prisoner had died and he was holding himself responsible. If only he had brought the over-worked medical officer's attention to him instead of doing what he thought was more urgent work, he might still be alive. How good to know dedication to healing rises above the horrors of hostilities.

When escorting the main fleet The Rookie would look forward to the force's final night at sea. Then, with action done, he would sit outside by the forecastle admiring the silhouettes of battleships, cruisers and an aircraft carrier. Ahead would be Alexandria, a run ashore and possibly a football match. Then, all too soon, another trip, air attacks and sinking ships. When would it all end?

As it turned out, the next assignment was for *Nubian* and *Mohawk*, the Eastern Mediterranean's only Tribal-class destroyers, to join *Jervis* and *Janus* in Malta and complete a striking force to bombard the enemy's North African coast in support of Wavell's Eighth Army. The bombardment soon became routine. Each ship contained a Captain of Commander rank and in addition, *Jervis* housed Captain Mack 14th in overall command. The tactics never varied. Once at sea the force formed a straight line, D14 leading in *Jervis*, next came *Janus* followed by the big girls *Nubian* number three and the tail ender batting at number four, *Mohawk*. The ships would charge at full speed straight at the enemy coast, turn at right angles and, once parallel with the coast fire as many salvoes as possible before turning seaward to face out of range of enemy gunfire. Enemy shells were always seen falling, but their guns were never visible. After assessment results and exchanging signals with Army control the force would then prepare for another 'run in'. So it went on until it came to return to Malta.

During intervals between bombardments "B" gun's crew relaxed by telling stories. For example the cockney wit was going to invent a dual purpose helmet used on the head for attacks by aircraft and on the backside for attacks by submarines. The Cornishman told of an amorous fisherman who in summer specialised in entertaining holiday-makers. His top jacket pocket contained a hunter pocket watch, beneath the front flap of which was concealed a condom. From the cliff top overlooking the sea he would show his girlfriend the setting sun and they would walk together over said dunes before arriving at the local inn, where his cronies would be given the precise time or told to get stuffed. The Captain occasionally looked down from the bridge when everyone was laughing.

What made "B" gun's crew tick? Why was an un-commissioned Rookie accepted as their 'officer in Action?' True, he once got a disciplinary offence against one crew member quashed. Nothing was ever mentioned but they knew, every member of every gun's crew knew. Whatever the reason an affinity was unmistakable. The cockney wit too played his part, always cheerful, indomitable in spirit and with a personality strong enough to keep the crew together.

The ship was bombarding when a faulty cordite container jammed the barrel of "B" gun mounting's starboard gun, resulting in firing rounds being missed. In frustration, the troublesome canister was removed and thrown overboard and the gun then fired merrily away. Later, with courtesy, the incident was mentioned to the Petty Officer in charge of ammunition and he was horrified.

"You cannot do that!" he said. "The number of shells must always equal the number of cordite canisters and ours do not. You civvies are all the same, you think ammunition comes by the barrow-load, when in fact every single piece must be accounted for. The only answer is to secretly drop one shell over the side, then everything will balance". This was done.

"That finalises that," said the PO.

"Not exactly," said the civvy. "Have you not forgotten the most important thing of all? Please, may I have a chit?"

The Captain's valet was a senior member of the Maltese Rating's Mess and went to his station when the alarm bells sounded. These were unexpected because the ship was beyond the danger zone and almost back home. With everyone at action stations the first announcement was made "The ship will return to normal working. Does that old Maltese fool not know the difference between enemy planes and seagulls?".

In 1941 the Wednesday of Holy Week came on April 16th and liberty men ashore were being recalled to their ships. A convoy of five Italian merchant ships, escorted by three destroyers, was reported to have left Italy and was heading for North Africa. Early that evening the four Malta-based destroyers, all with ship's companies honed to razor sharpness by repeated bombardments, sailed from Grand Harbour, Valletta, in line ahead and in search of the enemy.

Three hours later the enemy was sighted but everything was wrong. D14 was on the eastern side of, and going in to the same direction as, the convoy. He was also on the sky's lighter side, making it easier for the enemy's look out. The Malta-based destroyers were then swung round to make a seaward semi-circle at top speed and then put line ahead below the darker sky and on course, which would take them between the Tunisian coast and the enemy convoy. Now, everything was right, so even before the fireworks began one side was ahead on points; D14 was the one dictating terms. Battle ensigns were already flying from the ship's mainmasts. In surface actions HM ships flew two white ensigns in case one was destroyed by enemy action.

The Rookie, his authority unquestioned, his men ready, was standing by "B" gun mounting below the bridge, looking straight ahead and watching the gap between friend and foe get smaller. On his head was a tin hat, or "battle bowler", across his chest an inflatable life-belt similar in appearance to half a car tyre with fitted blow pipe, a cotton loop over the head and tapes at each end taken around the body to be tied above the navel. In one pocket were a school compass, a tourniquet and a small tin box containing morphine tubes, each with attached injection needle protected by a sealed glass capsule. Directions for use had long been memorised: break glass, inject casualty, write capital 'M' on his forehead, call doctor (always assuming the number of casualties equals the number of doctors). In another pocket were a 1910 Edwardian golden half-guinea piece, a few Victorian and Edwardian silver coins and some current paper money, all made watertight against the sea by a knotted sick-bay appliance. Gold, silver and the law of survival! Strapped to his wrist was an aluminium identity disc with name, rank, official number and blood group, and looped around his waist, easily detachable, was a navy-issue knife – releasing life rafts for the use of.

With the two leading destroyers almost adjacent with the convoy he saw bright sparks from a small machine gun on an enemy's destroyer's bridge. Immediately *Jervis* and *Janus* fired their first salvoes. Now, what the hell was happening? *Jervis* and *Janus* firing their guts out and the Tribals running away – actually running away – ahead of the bows nothing but open sea and the horizon. What a shambles!

The enemy commander not liking his ships being fired on began to take evasive action by turning seawards away from the coast. D14 had seen this possibility and had directed his tribals to an ideal position with all guns primed and raring to go. Brilliant! Absolutely bloody brilliant!

During the battle the Rookie had been concentrating deeply, watching the men working with precision, standing by to relieve anyone if needed, ensuring ejected cordite canisters did not impede gun loaders and generally acting as overseer. All he saw was his men and their guns. At no time had he been afraid and when the ceasefire order came he could have gone on longer.

Looking up for the time he saw several ships on fire. His eyes saw one explode, sending a massive ball of flame sky-high. When this subsided the ship's skeleton could be seen, cherry red from the heat and sinking below the sea; a remarkable sight.

He did not know what action the enemy had taken against *Nubian*; if shells and torpedoes had been aimed at her, nor did he know that *Mohawk* had been sunk by torpedoes from the *Tarigo*. This meant that *Nubian* must have held one flank alone.

For the enemy it was worse. Five merchant ships laden with troops, tanks, vehicles, ammunition and petrol, together with escorting destroyers *Tarigo*, *Lamp* and *Belino* had all been sunk.

D14 then sent his ships to get the *Mohawk*'s survivors and the Rookie left his station to go along to the grabbing nets. The navigating officer, worried about the tide, was afraid the ships would run aground, but luck favoured D14 and, with survivors on each ship he set sail for home – Malta.

It soon became established that on *Nubian* every man had done his job without trouble or mistakes. The ship had done its captain, its makers and its country proud.

When drawn broke on Thursday 17th April 1941 men were begging to assemble on the jetties around Grand Harbour, Valletta. Their numbers were growing each minute as the ships were sighted, heading directly towards them. The observant ones began to notice that the ships numbered three, not four, and each ship was flying two white ensigns. As D14 entered Grand Harbour leading his tailless destroyers, each with battle engines flying on the mainmasts, men whose courage and tenacity was later being admired by the whole world, crowds were there in their hundreds and hundreds and were waving and cheering and clapping, and D14's men were waving back and feeling good at being given an ecstatic reception by, of all people, the men of Malta. It was really something.

D14 called the action 'The Skirmish of Sfax'. Heaven knows what the Italians called it! During the following days the ship's company was one big happy family with complete absence of discord and animosity.

Then, later, there appeared our honours list. *Nubian's* share was three DSCs for officers and four DSMs for ratings, plus a number of 'mentions in dispatches'. Some senior and chief petty officers were disappointed and upset at being overlooked and cracks like "see you in Buckingham Palace" were not popular. The seaman's messes were also disappointed. One member said the medals had all been won by the ship and should have been put in a hat and drawn for. Another said if a medal owner died it should be passed on to someone else, like they do with Lords! Those old bastards have not got long to live anyhow!

The captain had, in fact, done a very good job. All captains similarly placed consult their senior officers before making a final decision and this, ironically, can be an unenviable task. In the unlikely event of the Rookie's opinion being invited he would simply have suggested the fourth choice DSM be exchanged with the chief ordinance officer mentioned in dispatches. It would have been explained to him that the chief OA already had one mention in despatches but two months previously had been a 'naughty boy' on shore leave in Alexandria. The Army Provost Marshal's report had reached the ship and the captain had to deal with it and ship's captains do not like having to apologise to the Army. The rookie was with him at the time and with football fitness had moved quicker and gone farther than the heavily booted leading runner of the military police patrol. In all honesty he could not say the damning report was unjustified. On the contrary, his punishment could have been much worse, but at least it would have been worth a try.

In retrospect, nigh on half a century of years in a changing world later it may seem that with the luxury of a potential four DSMs to play with, a free ship's lottery with the first prize a possible DSM and a second prize a 'mention in despatches' would have been a good investment in the boosting of morale and also empathy. What an opportunity the captain missed!

On May 20th 1941 Germany invaded Crete and it being an Eastern Mediterranean island like Malta all developments were carefully monitored. D14, already at sea on other business, was immediately diverted with his destroyers to positions between Greece and Crete and they were amongst the first ships in action. *Nubian*'s captain soon discovered to his displeasure two things. One, the enemy's high-level bombers had demoralising screaming devices attached to their bombs, and two, once a Stuka bomber began its dive onto the ship's stern the only defence was to take evasive action. The sternmost funnel prevented both Pom-Pom and rapid fire guns from bearing on the target and the 39½ degrees maximum elevation of the 4.7-inch main armament guns was insufficient against dive bombers. The enemy's homework had been done and the Tribals' 'blind spot' had been exposed.

Air General Freiherr von Richthofen, a nephew of World War I air ace, had amassed a strike force of 228 bombers, 205 dive bombers, 144 twin-engined fighters, 119 single-engined fighters and 50 spotter aircraft. Against these our air cover was virtually non-existent.

On day one both sides were warming up – a caique laden with soldiers was sunk by *Nubian*. What looked like countless planes were actually planes towing gliders, and air attacks began to get more frequent.

If seen before its dive a Stuka was not a serious threat but when synchronised with a high-level attack it was. After the dive, in theory, a Stuka became a 'sitting duck' target, but it then flew between ships, inviting them to fire on each other. Also, it being expedient to concentrate on incoming rather than outgoing raiders, a high percentage were getting away with it.

The ship was at action stations throughout the second day. Rum rations were brought around and the NAFFI canteen manager appeared with his wares in biscuit tins. One PO wanted a good clear out. Toilets were in darkness with portholes closed and tungsten filaments in electric light bulbs fractured by the ship's violent battering. A near miss by a screaming bomb came down and out he came clutching his lifebelt with his trousers down. A fine state of affairs when one cannot answer a call of nature in peace!

On the following day the Rookie received his only compliment of the war and also went through his most traumatic experience. Waist deep in water he got a badly wounded survivor safely up the grabbing nets. The first lieutenant, calling him by name, said "We'll Done!" Next came the trouble with the foremost gun mounting; a strained safety cam prevented it being loaded. The crew were deployed, leaving the chief PO and his understudy alone with the troublesome gun. Bombing was intense, the ship was fighting like a cornered rat and the chief OA was bleeding and knocked out.

What to do? First get medical help, then continue with repairs. After three yards another bomb; down went the rookie, lying face downwards with compacted cotton waste between closed eyes and the deck. His chief may roll overboard and he would be charged with manslaughter. Another few yards and down again, this time surely a hit, but no, a very close miss, If hit or killed in this position he will be accused of running away and branded a coward. Eventually the sick bay was reached and, unable to talk, he led the medical PO to the forecastle where the chief OA was alive and conscious.

On that single day the junior OA ceased to be a boy and became a man, albeit a frightened and devastated man.

Being one of the first ships in the battle *Nubian* was amongst the first to run dangerously short of ammunition and made a dash to Alexandria where casualties, including the chief OA were taken off, ammunition replenished and the crew rested before returning to action.

When back off Crete the ship joined the force of Rear Admiral King commanding Australian cruisers *Naidd* and *Perth,* RN cruisers *Calcutta* and *Carlisle,* and destroyers *Kandahar, Kingston* and *Nubian.*

Resulting from post war differences this report moves on to the time when *Nubian* was seriously damaged and expected to sink.

With all ship's guns firing a Stuka bomber scored a direct hit on the stern. The Rookie, by the foremost guns, turned to see flames reaching skyward. Unbelievably cool and in self-control he advised gun crew members to prepare to abandon ship. Experience had shown that similarly damaged ships sank stern first, their bows pointing vertically upwards before slowly sinking. By then an urgent order to throw everything available overboard was broadcast. Four unprimed torpedoes were first to go, followed by everything down to the Officers laundry. The ship was going to resist sinking. Another destroyer was detailed as escort and the fight for survival was on…

Thinking he could help the Rookie went to the disaster area. He looked down upon a scalp from which came streaks of red, ending in coagulated blobs of blood. His eyes were transfixed, he began to shake and then went back for'ard – may God forgive him! Later corpses and parts of corpses were being buried at sea. The first lieutenant began reading a service but could not continue and the prayer book was taken from him by the gunnery officer – the only commissioned man on board from the lower deck.

Remembering the scalp the rookie felt a little less guilty.

A grim sight presented itself to anyone looking down from the PO's mess. Wounded men were lying on stretchers on tables and on deck.

Others, more fortunate, were holding up bottles of plasma with transfusion tubes connected to casualties. In addition to normal duties seamen organised their own tending rotas and no wounded man was left unattended. Working selflessly away was the medical officer – a giant of a man in every respect. Thank god he himself was not a casualty. Feeling completely inadequate the Rookie went over to where the cockney wit, weary from lack of sleep, was on tending duty.

"Now, don't you worry chief," he said. "We shall make it. Go and get some fresh air." What a man!

The Rookie went outside and sat by the forecastle. On the bridge a lonely captain was praying he would not have to press the 'abandon ship' button. Down in the engine room artificers and stokers were doing sterling work under extremely difficult conditions and, on the mess decks-cum-hospital the medical officer was working to save lives. Every minute of every hour the safety of Alexandria was drawing closer. The escort destroyer, herself short of ammunition, was keeping vigil. The darkness of night was shielding the ships from enemy spotter planes. The sea was friendly and trying to stay calm and, most of all, the ship was refusing to sink and put her men at risk.

Against advice the Rookie was unable to stop thinking of the gun's crew he had known and joked with, two of whom, being ambitious had sought his help when preparing for their Navy Higher Educational test. One had played alongside him in the ship's football team and once a complete misunderstanding between the two had resulted in the opposing side scoring a goal. They had blamed each other and now ... Oh My God ... and now ...

Not known at the time was that two further DSCs and three DSMs were to be awarded, all won on merit and not begrudged. The first lieutenant, sent down from the bridge by the captain, took charge of the disaster area, made big decision and succeeded in getting the situation under control. He was awarded a Bar to his Sfax DSC. The medical officer, despite screaming and diving bombs, spent hours on bended knees massaging the captain's legs to keep him going. The man, without whose skill and selfless devotion the ship's obituary list would have undoubtedly been longer, was awarded the DSC. The Rotherham gun loader, adjudged the ship's most seriously wounded casualty and the one nearest the explosion to survive, recovered sufficiently to be sent home. Thank you sir! The chief engine room artificer and the senior ERA did good work keeping the boilers and engines going under extremely difficult conditions and worked themselves to the point of exhaustion. For the chief a bar to his Sfax DSM and for his senior assistant a DSM. The sick bay PO, disregarding his own safety, dived overboard and rescued four separate wounded survivors, all of whom lived; for him a DSM.

On June 1st 1941 Crete was evacuated. All that remained was to count the cost. For the Navy alone this was frightening. Three cruisers and six destroyers sunk, others seriously damaged and needing prolonged repairs. Also two battleships and one aircraft carrier damaged by direct hits.

The casualty figures, 2000 sailors killed. Statistically round figures are suspect; if taken to the nearest 100 the figure could be 2049; to the nearest thousand 2499. Many more were seriously wounded, some for life.

Without doubt a disaster, a nightmare, but, in the Rookie's view it could have been worse. Had the Italian fleet come out and positioned itself between Crete and Alexandria, with the enemy commanding the air and our ships low on ammunition and with exhausted crews, the results could have been catastrophic. Perhaps liaison between Germany and Italy was suspect, or maybe the effects of Calabria, Taranto, Matapan and to a lesser extent Sfax had been more momentous than realised. Of his ships and men the Commander in chief used the words: "Never So Proud".

Years later came an unexpected body blow. Viscount Cunningham of Hyndhore in *A Sailor's Odyssey* criticised Rear Admiral King (not commanders of other sections), implying his tactics should have been more audacious. Naval tactics at this level are beyond the Rookie's depth so he cannot comment, but one thing for sure he knows, that did HURT!

Not being Malta-related, the following points are now stated, not described.

7.12.41 Japanese war planes attacked American warships at Pearl Harbour. Germany declared war on the U.S.A. Churchill slept well.

24.8.42 Completed 2½ years on striking destroyer; now due for relief.

A month or so later "This is your Captain speaking. Our ship is now the sole survivor of the first flotilla of tribal class destroyers and in consequence we shall call ourselves "The Avenger". The ship's company, like Queen Victoria, was not amused.

9.10.42 completed three years in the Royal Navy. Promoted from A4 (Petty Officer Rank) to OA3 (Chief PO rank). Moved into CPO's mess. Accommodation better but remote from seamens messes and close liaison with gun's crews is more difficult. Ship now has twin 0.4-inch gun mounting with elevation of 80 degrees no less and Oerlikon AA guns at key points. The 'blind spot' has been rectified. The next stepping stone will be on **17.11.42** – my twenty-fourth birthday.

On 17th November 1942 the ship reached Alexandria from Port Said. A birthday celebration ashore was planned and rumour suggested my relief was already here and available for transfer. Then a shock announcement: the ship was under sailing orders and all leave was cancelled.

Later that day four merchant ships with a screen of destroyers of which *Nubian* was one were at sea bound for Malta. The briefing was simple, despite expected heavy air attacks it was imperative for at least one merchant ship to arrive intact. Day after day the expected air attacks did not materialise and, unbelievably, the whole convoy arrived unmolested, which was just as well because on that day Malta's reserves of foodstuffs, ammunition and aviation spirit were down to thirteen days.

To supplement the Merchant ship's supplies all destroyers unloaded virtually all their foodstuffs, leaving on board just sufficient to cover their return to Alexandria. Then emerged a new plan – the destroyers were not to return to Alexandria but stay in Malta as an offensive striking force. They were immediately put on basic siege rations.

It was known that the enemy was short of petrol, so when a report of a convoy, including a tanker, heading for North Africa was received the destroyers raced off at full speed. But Alas! RAF Bombers were first on the scene and left only one undamaged destroyer which was going round in circles picking up survivors and, in the dark of night, exposed itself by slowly passing between a blazing ship and the oncoming Malta-based destroyers. Of its captain it could be said: "He did not fight and run away, to fight again another day". In the one-sided action which followed he was sunk.

For the handful of men whose time on board dated back to "The Skirmish off Sfax" this was an anti-climax. However one enemy destroyer was worth going out for, for untried gun's crews it was excellent combat experience and for the new captain a step on the road to his DSO. At about this time, to the Rookie's discredit, his morale began to weaken. Tired, hungry, more than three months overdue for relief and still regarding himself as being on loan to the industry, he lacked the resilience of hardened continuous service professionals. Strangely he began to feel out of place with a young and fresh ship's company thirsting for action.

In all wars events happen quickly and unexpectedly, and on December 6th 1942 a convoy suddenly appeared in harbour. The Rookie ordnance artificer and the electrical artificer were sent for, told their reliefs were here and ordered to start packing. The transfer from ship to the chief and PO's mess in barracks was so swift that no thought had been given to the matter of getting off the island. When consulted the mess chairman said most probably it would be either by flying or by submarine.

The artificers soon fitted into their new surroundings. The mess members, some of whom were survivors, were amused at the speed with which we hurried for shelter every time an air raid siren sounded.

The briefing envelope arrived. The artificers were to report at the airport no later than midnight. One luggage case only was permitted. Everything else, kitbags, hammocks, tools, etc had to be left behind. Old clothes were readily accepted by survivors, all tobacco was sold at basic tax free rates and one survivor, delighted at being given a fancy issue attaché case, insisted on giving the artificers a tot of rum, virtually his sole asset.

At the airport the naval artificers joined a group of men who were standing up and were sufficient in number to fill half a tennis court. After careful weighing all were packed into the bomb bay of a Liberator bomber due to fly out to Gibraltar at 4am. First on board were army officers, followed by CPO artificers, who were ahead of 'odd bods' of lower rank.

Once airborne it became intensely cold. The two most senior army officers were sat foremost facing each other beneath the plane's nose and for them body heat transfer was restricted to one side only and their places were by far the coldest on board. The bomb bay of an RAF liberator bomber had little respect for the privilege of priority.

A few hours later, by which time their life expectancy years had been reduced, the passengers were met on arrival and taken to their respective barracks. In Gibraltar during the next few days two naval artificers whose efforts for Malta had just been a 'drop in the ocean' were living well, eating every two hours, frequenting bars with unlimited supplies of beer, wines and spirits and unaware of reactions still to come.

Finally when year 1942 drew to its close and gave way to a new year 1943, an East Midland coal mining village contained one, hostilities only, Chief Petty Officer ordnance artificer who had arrived on boxing day with gastroenteritis, a complete lack of appetite and whose only luggage had been lost in transit. He found its inhabitants had vocabularies which appeared to consist entirely of the words 'older' and 'thinner'. His mother while delighted to have him home realised the days of ever seeing her son young and carefree again – like the days of the siege of Malta – were over.

POSTSCRIPT

On September 8th 1943 Italy surrendered. For Malta the price had been catastrophically high. In the city of Senglea alone a frightening 80% of all buildings had been demolished; many others were damaged, some uninhabitable. Display your George Cross with pride folks, the world knows you earned it!

Italian warships with white flags began to trickle into the harbours of Valletta. When the figure reached a staggering sixty five, Admiral Sir Andrew Cunningham sent his historic message to the Admiralty of London. It read:

"Please to inform their Lordships that the Italian Battle Fleet now rests at anchor under the guns of the Fortress of Malta".

The drops in the ocean had done their job.

The *Nubian* continued on her adventurous way and, despite numerous attacks on her, survived the war. Eventually, her useful life over, she who refused to sink in war went in peace to the breakers yard with head held high. Her name was inherited by a new frigate.

The Rookie was later commissioned and became an Electrical officer attached to the Fleet Air Arm. By this time he was reasonably proficient at naval ordnance, had forgotten most of his electro technology, knew absolutely nothing about aeroplanes, and had to start all over again. He is believed to have been the only man in the World War II to have held the ranks of ordnance officer and electrical officer. He would like to thank Malta's own Joseph Attard from whose book *Battle of Malta* some facts, figures and names of Italian ships were taken.

THE FINAL ROUND

Late in 1945 with the war in Europe and the Far East over, a Southport Billionaire industrialist was having a party. Invited were RNVR officers from the nearby Fleet Air Arm station who were there awaiting demobilisation. Off they went to the party, leaving behind the solitary figure of the duty officer of the day. But pity him not, after all he had seen service in Malta and had also done some forward planning. Once the coast was clear he went along to the telephone exchange and saw the switchboard operator. Explaining the position and leaving a number to be alerted, he then tried to find if the station's duty van could find its way to the party.

On the following day, looking and feeling terrible, he went with a hangover and a block of NAAFI 'nutty' chocolate to thank the duty Wren for her co-operation. She was annoyed, very annoyed.

"Look at you! Just look at the state you are in!" she said. "Well I have news for you, my lad … I plan to straighten you out. I am going to marry you!"

On dear! Oh Dear! He thought he had got away with it.

But what happened?

Now when all is said and done,
The Rookie lost, the Wren won!

22. THE GEORGE CROSS PRESENTATION

Compiled from official records by Frank Rixon BEM

The George Cross was awarded to Malta by King George VI in a message to General Dobbie dated 15 April 1942:

THE CITATION

"To honour her brave people I award the George Cross
to the Island Fortress of Malta
to bear witness to a heroism and devotion
that will long be remembered."

Because of the prevailing circumstances the actual presentation could not take place until Sunday the 13 of September 1942 and even this was kept secret from the outside world for security reasons. The presentation ceremony took place on the Palace Square with rubble piled high from the damaged buildings. Detachments of the Navy, Army, Police, Special Constabulary, and Passive Defence Organisations all took part. The Police Commissioner Joseph Axisa handed the case containing the G.C. to Lord Gort, who had by this time replaced General Dobbie, and he addressed the parade as follows:

"On my appointment as Governor of Malta I was entrusted to carry the George Cross to this Island Fortress. By Command of the King I now present to the people of Malta and its Dependencies the decoration which his Majesty has awarded to them in recognition of the gallant service which they have already rendered in the fight for freedom. How you have withstood for many months the most concentrated attacks in history of the world is the admiration of all civilised people. Your

homes and your historic buildings have been destroyed and only the ruins remain as monuments to the hate of a barbarous foe. The Axis Powers have tried again and again to break your spirit but your confidence in the final triumph of the United Nations remains undimmed. What Malta has stood without flinching, Malta is determined to endure until the day when the second siege is raised. Battle-scarred George Cross Malta, the sentinel of the Empire in the Mediterranean meanwhile stands firm, undaunted, un-dismayed and awaiting the time when she can call "Pass Friend, all is well in the Island Fortress". Now it is my proud duty to hand over the George Cross to the people of Malta for Safe Keeping"

Lord Gort then read out the Citation. His Honour Sir George Borg received the award and after an address the George Cross was placed on a plinth to be guarded by the 1st Battalion the Kings Own Malta Regiment.

Lord Gort and the Chief Justice at the presentation of the George Cross.

Lord Gort presenting the George Cross to the Chief Justice.

Guard of Honour by 1st Bn, the Kings Own Malta Regiment.

Malta's George Cross

23. THE FAST MINELAYERS

A.G, Evans RN - HMS Abdiel

The fast minelaying class of ship had four units built by the beginning of World War Two. They were HMS *Abdiel*, HMS *Latonia*, HMS *Welshman* and HMS *Manxman* and a further two were under construction: HMS *Apollo* and HMS *Ariadne*. This small group of secret ships which always worked alone and at great speed in an area closed by the enemy to normal Royal Navy units began their task of laying mines at the edge of the desert where Rommel unloaded his men, provisions and necessary war supplies. Their task of minelaying completed, these small but speedy ships were only too ready to fight their way back to safer waters.

The design of the fast minelayer despatched around the German fleet to lay mines in the track they would follow to return to their base. The mission she successfully completed and she returned to her base.

Despite the criticisms of many of Hitler's plans, one of his strategies was sound: The Atlantic Wall. This was a plan to stabilise the Russian Front, remove the Royal Navy from the Mediterranean and the British Army from Africa. His plan was that after invading Spain he would then have an uninterrupted front from the North to South Poles.

There were, however, four flies in the ointment, the Royal Navy's fast minelayers, the fastest ships in the world at the time, capable of over 50mph. The fate of the British Eighth Army in North Africa depended on them interrupting the enemy supply lines. They did not fail in this mission; the sunk so many German troop ships, supply ships and fuel tankers that the bottom of the Med was littered with them. When there was too much moonlight for minelaying operations they switched to making supply runs to Malta and Tobruk, carrying much-needed stores, food and ammunition. There was no let up for these small but sturdy craft.

Sadly, by the law of averages, they were all in time doomed, having had one of the most dangerous tasks of the whole war. The first of these gallant ships to go was HMS *Latonia,* sunk off Bardia during a night air attack; struck in the engine room by a 250lb bomb which also set fire to her cargo of ammunition bound for Tobruk. Once her crew had abandoned her she was sunk by a torpedo from the escorting HMS *Encounter.*

Approximately 12 months later HMS *Manxman* was caught and torpedoed by a U-Boat on the Tunisian coast. At great risk she was expertly floated and coaxed by superb seamanship to dry dock in Gibraltar and later was able to undergo refitting in the United Kingdom. *Manxman* then survived until the end of the war.

On 1st October 1942 fate caught up with HMS *Welshman.* After sterling work she was torpedoed by a pack of U-Boats now known to have been lying in wait for her. At least one enemy cruiser was also stationed in the area. The *Welshman* was loved and missed by the people of Malta, whom she had served so well, bringing much-needed stores and supplies.

While HMS *Welshman* was well known in Malta, we in her sister ship HMS *Abdiel* only made an occasional visit during the Siege. The nature of our operations made it necessary to pass through the dangerous waters around Malta when we were attacking Rommel's supply lines. One night we found ourselves surrounded by E-Boats with our load of explosive mines still on board. There was a short, sharp engagement and we made our escape, but this made us late to meet up with our escort of cruisers in the morning, so our captain decided to run for Malta to hide out during daylight hours. The news was round the island in a jiffy that a ship was coming in and the people lined the walls to cheer us in. But alas, we hardly had anything to give them. We landed what we could and slipped away in the evening, a most heartbreaking experience.

We were secret vessels, working alone, so we knew little of the activities of the rest of the squadron. However, I have reason to believe that Malta thinks well of the fast minelayers.

The loss of HMS *Welshman* left HMS *Abdiel* as the sole operating fast minelayer unit and she carried out the responsibility of protecting the seaward side of the desert campaign with great distinction. Gradually, in part as a result of her and her sister ships efforts, the 8th Army was slowly gaining the upper hand and less operations were necessary to protect the land forces. This allowed *Abdiel* to take part in the Sicily landings, where she proudly wore the three union flags of the Commander in Chief-Royal Navy, Army and RAF, as their Command Ship.

Later on, HMS *Abdiel* was at rest in Malta; a very well-deserved rest, one might add. Malta was gradually getting back to normal after the long siege because the 8th Army had proved victorious in the desert. The ship was the sole remaining unit of a squadron of four fast minelayers working in close support of the military operations. Life was idyllic: plenty of swimming over the side, rest, and most important of all, plenty of sleep.

When the public address system announced that Petty Officer Evans was required to report to the 1st Lieutenant in his cabin he trotted along to see what it was all about. Boredom was beginning to creep in, except perhaps for "Taff' Stringer, who was acting junior PO and coxswain of the motorboat and thus had a regular harbour job. That left Evans to take emergencies. Lt Commander Harry Westacott was a gentleman and had a way of giving you an order so that you felt in carrying it out you were doing him a personal favour. Apparently the Maltese Dockyard had gone on strike. Something big was in the wind and it was imperative that all the destroyers that crammed Sliema Creek had to be topped up with fresh water on that day. It gave Evans a pleasant feeling as a newly-promoted mate; he was in charge of a grizzled ERA as engineer and some ABs and stokers as crew of the Admiralty Water Ship with a Sub-Lt as skipper. They soon had the feel of the ship and as they moved from boat to boat like a milk cow Evans could hardly believe he knew so many people, mostly ex-HMS *Ganges*, with many senior ratings making pressing invitations to partake of rum 'snippers' with a friendly "Come aboard Taff".

On one ship he happened to see his old 'oppo' Ginger Cattle, a diver, engrossed in making a 'prick' of tobacco. He was liberally dosing the leaf with neat rum, but when he made to toss the leftovers over the guard rail Evans hastily made to restrain him.

"But it's had my fingers in it Taff!"

"I don't care if it's had something worse in it, you can't throw it away!"

"No problem Taff. Come inside."

Going back to the victualling wharf the empty ship minus the ballast of water it had delivered had its bows high out of the water and was quite unmanageable. Duly moored and secured the scratch crew had but one problem. How to smuggle one mumbling and incoherent Mate back on board and stick him in his hammock.

Next morning the ships had gone; off to the beaches of Sicily.

During this campaign HMS *Abdiel* came to her end. In the early hours of 10th September 1943, packed with paratroopers and anti-tank guns, she was blown in two, ironically by a mine, whilst in harbour at Taranto, Italy. The 10th September was the very first day that allied soldiers landed back on the mainland of Europe. She and her sister ships of the Royal Navy Fast Minelayers had lived up to Abdiel's motto: "*Semper Fidelis*" (Ever faithful).

It is not surprising therefore that the Royal Navy personnel who served on these ships consider themselves not only part of the marine battles but also key figures in the Mediterranean and Desert campaigns.

ROYAL NAVY FAST MINELAYER CASUALTIES

Ship	Date	How Lost	Killed	Wounded
HMS *Latona*	25/10/1941	Air Attack; 250 lb bomb	20	1
HMS *Welshman*	01/02/1943	Torpedo	118[3]	
HMS *Abdiel*	10/09/1943	Mine	48	1
HMS *Manxman*	01/12/1942	Torpedo. Survived the war		

[3] included 107 paratroopers of 6th Welsh Fusiliers.

24. NEVER LOSE YOUR HEAD

Richard McDonald – 7HAA Regt, RA

On a sunny Friday morning in Malta in April 1942 I was a L/Bdr who happened to be in charge of the guard that morning. A very large enemy raid was taking place and there were many enemy planes around. They came in from the north and started to dive from the edge of the island towards Luqa flying directly over our position at Tal Handak.

One of the JU88s was hit and the crew started to bail out; one of them dropped into the field next to Tal Handak. Word got to me at the Guard Room about 10 minutes afterwards.

"A German airman has dropped nearby," someone said. "Like to go and have a look at him?"

"OK," I said, and after putting someone in charge of the Guard I went over to the field to take a look. Teddy Rose was already there and had put a blanket over the German. He uncovered him when I arrived.

"A ghastly sight, McDonald, isn't it?" he said.

It was indeed a horrible sight. He must have been hit by shrapnel on his way down because he had been completely decapitated.

"Where is his head?" I asked.

"We don't know. It must be knocking about somewhere…"

He must have been in his early twenties and was quite a sturdily built chap. He had on a khaki uniform with an eagle and a swastika on it. I went back to the Guard Room and related what I had seen. Eventually they took the body away, down the road to HQ, and I thought no more about it.

I should add that at this time we were hungry in Malta, and when I say hungry, we really were. The rations were pretty meagre. We were allowed three ounces of flour a week and nine ounces bread a day (the civilians only got three). Nine ounces is not much for breakfast, dinner, tea and supper. Bacon came in tins about the size of an evaporated milk tin, rolled in cellophane paper; one tin between 12 men for breakfast. Cauliflower, I remember was four to 100 men – you didn't get much cauliflower! There were plenty of artichokes and lentils; when I say plenty, I mean a spoonful. Dried potatoes came out grey and tea was innocent water scalded to death. These were but a few of the rations we had.

Anyway… we were hungry and there were fields of tomatoes, potatoes, grapes, peaches etc all around, so inevitably we did a bit of pinching but, of course, the farmers took umbrage at this and put up little tents in their fields in which they lay at night with their shotguns, ready to repel poachers, although they never actually shot any of us.

They weighed us every two weeks. When I came to Malta I was a healthy 12 stone 7lbs, no fat whatsoever, fit as a fiddle, playing football, boxing, etc. I went down to 10 stone 3lbs.

It was Friday and we used to get paid on Fridays but there was nothing to spend our money on, so on a Friday evening when we were off duty we organised a game of Pontoon in the Command Post concrete dugout and gambled with our wages. That night about eight of us were playing. We had to be careful in case one of the sergeants caught us, because we could be put on a 252 (charge sheet) for gambling, so when we heard someone approaching at around midnight we swept up all the money, put it in our pockets and carried on playing.

We looked around to see who was coming; it was Gunner O'Rourke. We all had a nickname in those days and his was 'Haystack'. He came from Newry in County Down. He was one of our regular players.

"Are you going to have a game of cards?" we asked.

"No," he said. "I shan't play tonight."

He walked up and with a swift movement took something from behind his back and plonked it down in the middle of the table in front of us.

"How about that?" he said.

It was a severed human head. The eyes were closed and the nose looked broken. The bottom jaw was completely gone and all the teeth from the top jaw were gone as well.

"Where the hell did you get that thing?" we said.

"I was out in the tomato field pinching some tomatoes," says Haystack, "and there he was, singing 'I ain't got no body'."

That comment had us all in stitches. It may seem callous to a modern-day reader, but after the pummelling we had been taking in Malta we felt no compassion for the Germans.

When I came home from Malta and went to Dublin I told lots of people this story, but I am afraid none of them would believe me. Perhaps they would have if they had known Gunner O'Rourke, who was always ready with a quip and was a great ad-libber.

About two months later our Medical Orderly, Bombardier Griffin took me to his bunk and said, "Have a look at this". He opened his soldiers' box and there he had an Iron Cross inscribed with the owner's name and rank and 'Poland 1939'. He told me it had belonged to the headless German aviator. Teddy also had his diary. We went through it together as I knew a bit of German. It turned out that it was this airman's third time over Malta. It also contained the addresses of some women in Vienna where he had been stationed.

Editors Note: It never fails to amaze me how many different stories have come out about the war and are in no official records that I know of.

25. A THREAT TOO FAR?

From the Album of Sgt H.J. Randall

In May 1942 there had been a lot of petty pilfering among the civilian and airfield workers at Takali aerodrome, which so infuriated the Station Commander, Wing Commander E.J. Gracie, that he had a gibbet erected beside the perimeter fence as a warning that all those who got caught would suffer the consequences. It is understood the *Daily Mirror* got hold of the picture in the UK and the Air Ministry got involved.

The question is "Would the sentence have been carried out?"

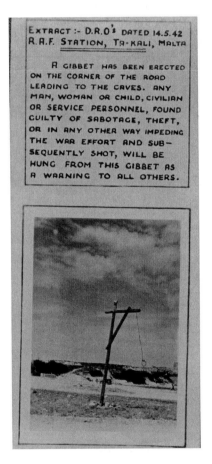

EXTRACT :- D.R.O's DATED 14.5.42
R.A.F. STATION, TA-KALI, MALTA

A GIBBET HAS BEEN ERECTED ON THE CORNER OF THE ROAD LEADING TO THE CAVES. ANY MAN, WOMAN OR CHILD, CIVILIAN OR SERVICE PERSONNEL, FOUND GUILTY OF SABOTAGE, THEFT, OR IN ANY OTHER WAY IMPEDING THE WAR EFFORT AND SUBSEQUENTLY SHOT, WILL BE HUNG FROM THIS GIBBET AS A WARNING TO ALL OTHERS.

26. A SECRET WEAPON

Jim Bellows - Royal Hampshire Regiment

I was in Valletta one day and met a rear gunner from the Fleet Air Arm and we got chatting. In the course of the conversation he said:

"Most of our flying is by night, looking for enemy convoys".

"How do you expect to find ships on a dark night?" I asked.

He laughed and said "Blues." (Blues was a bottled beer). "I take a couple of crates of empty bottles up with me in the rear cockpit." (They had no canopies on the cockpit of the Swordfish). "We cruise over the area where a convoy might be on its way to North Africa and throw a few bottles over the side. As they fall the air whistles from the mouth of the bottle and if there is a ship in the area and it has a nervous gunner on watch he will open fire and give its position away. The pilot then notifies Malta and then attacks with bombs or torpedoes, depending on what he is carrying. We then attack with machine guns blazing. The pilot makes another run and we tip the rest of the bottles over the side, hoping they will land on the deck of the ship and do a bit of damage. If you are lucky the bottles will explode like grenades and do a bit of damage, but of course we are not lucky every time."

I looked at him and said, "You are kidding!" but he swore it was true. [4]

---

[4] Editors Note: Fact is sometimes stranger than fiction!

27. TWO SHREWD POLITICIANS

Joseph Attard – 137 Maintenance Unit, Kalafrana, RAF

When uncommitted serving in the RAF I was stationed at 137 Maintenance Unit at Kalafrana in February 1943. One night when on duty the
sirens started wailing for an air-raid and I went to the window in expectation of the usual display of searchlights and exciting extravaganza of ack-
ack I had come to know so well. My expectation was short-lived, however,
when I was called to the Operations Room, where I was told the alert was
caused by a lone raider and that the enemy aircraft was transmitting in
plain language. Since I could speak Italian I was asked to make a transla-
tion. Indeed the enemy pilot was asking for lights to be shown so that he
could come down. By then orders had been coming in from higher-ups in
the Malta Defence set-up and since the enemy aircraft was identified as
being a Cant Seaplane, Kalafrana, which used to be a seaplane base and
still had light buoys was asked to accommodate the enemy. So we put on
the lights and sent out a boat with an armed party to wait for the enemy
aircraft.

The Italian seaplane came down and its crew of five was brought to my
office so that I could keep them company (as I could speak Italian) until
they could be taken away. I could hardly put in a word to the Italian Pilot
(a Capitano Pilota, equivalent to our Squadron Leader) who could not
stop blaspheming and blaming his navigator for having foolishly mistaken
Malta for Pantelleria. A spick and span Lieutenant ignored his captain's
ranting and engaged me in social conversation. He asked me where I lived
in Malta and when I told him he said he knew a girl from the same town.
He was not joking because when he told me her name I found out I knew
the girl myself! She had been studying in England and the Italian had met
her on the boat bringing them back on the declaration of war, because he
too was at that time studying at Oxford. It was then my turn to tell him off

for letting me continue a conversation in Italian when he obviously could speak Oxford English. Before he was taken away he asked me to express his regards to the girl when I saw her. It was years later that I met the girl and passed the message. She immediately remembered the Italian gentleman she had met on the boat, but when I told her that he had mistaken Malta for Pantelleria when navigating the aircraft, she laughed.

"I wouldn't be surprised if he had done it on purpose. He hated Mussolini so much and was not keen to fight for him."

My other story concerns Lord Gort, Governor and C-in-C at Malta during her worst war years… Two boys climbed into the grounds of St Anton Palace, the governor's residence, and went for the kitchen in search of some food. They found only a tin of corned beef and some hard biscuits. Before they could leave they were found by the cook, who raised hell and began calling the guard. It was, however, Lord Gort himself who turned up and asked the cook to let the boys go.

"I saw them climbing the wall from my window," said Lord Gort.

"So why did you not have them stopped?" said the surprised cook.

"Because I knew they were after food," replied Lord Gort, "and I wanted them to find out that their governor was living on the same kind and quantity of rations as the rest of the people."

28. H.M. Motor Launches

Lt Cmdr F.R. Price-Fox DSC, VRD and bar, RNR

In 1940/41 I was a Sub Lt RNVR Gunner Navigator on HMS *Azalea* (Kpts 25), part of Capt D13's Escort Group based at Gibraltar. In those days the Forecastle heads were the short version on the Flower Class Corvettes, and Negative Radar. Our Officer compliment was, a Lt RNR as CO, Canadian Sub RCNVR as 1st Lt and myself as Sub Lt RNVR (Ex Midshipman RNR J124 from HMS *Laurentic*, AMC of the 10th Cruiser Squadron).

Due to the continuous sea time of D13's Flotilla – we only returned to Gibraltar for refuelling and provisioning – stress and strain began to show on most of the officers in the Flotilla. Capt D13 (Bungy Williams) also was I/C Coastal Waters Forces at Gib, these comprised 8 Fairmile BMLs in the 3rd and 9th Flotillas, based on the old ISKA in the pens. As the MLs were only used on Bay Patrol, D13 had a wonderful idea. Change over officers between MLs and Corvettes for at least a three week round trip, thus giving the coastal boys some sea time, a rest cure for the Corvette types. I was transferred temporary to HMML130 and her two officers joined HMS *Azalea*, whose next trip was as an escort to an HG convoy, which took her home to the UK and a six months refit, to extend her forecastle to abaft the funnel and fit her out with radar.

ML130 lay alongside in the pens awaiting a replacement 12-cyl Hall Scott Engine to complete her quota of two engines, the other one had blown up (they ran on 87 octane fuel as used by the Gib Based Catalina a/c). The other officer with me was Lt David Jolly RNVR and he took command. Whilst waiting for the starboard engine the panic started when HMS *Ark Royal* was torpedoed and everything afloat in Gib was sailed to help with the rescue, some 50/70 miles east of the Rock.

ML130 was still alongside when D13 came charging down the dockside and ordered us to sea on one engine and as the hydraulics were stripped down, on hand steering from aft, by long wooden tiller. Quite fun on a twin screw boat, no lockhead power steering and only one engine and two officers who had never handled that boat before. By the time we arrived at the "Ark" all spare crew were taken off and she was being towed towards Gib by a pair of minesweeping trawlers. She had a horrible list to starboard and was on fire in the engine room. At about 0130 on 13 Nov 41 it was decided to abandon her and I was ordered to go alongside under the listing forward flight deck overhang and take off the towing party. Good job it was dark and very few saw the problems we had executing that manoeuvre, but we did it and as we pulled away, lopsided with a deck cargo of 30-40 towing party a thunderous crash saw the flight deck overhang break off and crash into the sea. TOO close for comfort!

At about 0230 we transferred the party to a destroyer and all the MLs were left at the scene to rescue and salvage anything that came up from the *Ark* after breaking up down below. Have you ever heard an extraordinarily large floater scrambling net come up to the surface from 200 odd fathoms deep? Its just like an express train coming at you from a tunnel and shooting up a hundred feet into the air before crashing down alongside. The same for balks of timber 12-15 inches square by 15-20 feet long and so heavy that we could not get them on deck, so we towed them back to the dockyard at Gib.

Eventually, after that and other fiascos we acquired our missing engine and along with the rest of the 3rd we were fitted out with five extra upper deck fuel tanks. From memory these measured four feet square by twelve feet long. These in turn had to be fitted with ladders at each end and duckboards on the upper surface, complete with guard rails. Over the below decks fuel compartment were fitted a bandstand and 20mm Oerlikon gun, this encompassed the full width of the boat, so you can imagine the hazard of moving around from fore to aft with all these death traps!

To complete the picture of utter chaos we were issued with parcels of hardboard and plywood with odd bits of canvas which turned out to be material to alter silhouette and create camouflage and 'fool the enemy'! The Flotilla put to sea in daylight and headed out into the Atlantic and performed various anti-submarine exercises. After dusk fell we were paired off and under cover of darkness headed east through the Straits at roughly two hourly intervals. The leading couple were 130 and 126 and were the only boats to complete the trip first time and in seven days. The remainder of the flotilla had to give up the ghost and eventually made the trip some 8 or 10 months later.

Meanwhile, proceeding eastwards in daylight off the French held land we flew the Spanish Ensign, off Italian ground we flew the French flag and during the last couple of days when Italian aircraft appeared we hoisted the German Naval Ensign and had air escort for about two hours!

The last day of our eastbound trip we lay alongside a wrecked German Merchantman, lying with 'tween' decks awash and on Kirkenha Banks (off Sfax), it being our intention to do the last 60/70 miles under the cover of darkness and arrive in Malta at dawn. During the night alongside the German freighter we heard odd noises coming from inboard, so we cleared lower decks and issued the full ships company with every type of weapon we could muster, two 1914 rifles, two pistols, four carving knives, two galley choppers, plus two hammers and at the order. "Away Boarders" all twelve of us went aboard the freighter and felt really bloodthirsty. After a diligent search from forward to aft we eventually found a bunch of four Arabs who apparently were left on board the many wrecks to salvage copper, brass etc. A "mother ship" collected the booty once a week.

During our rounding up of these Worthy Oriental Gentlemen in the half light between decks one of them threw a knife in our direction and we responded by firing one round over their heads from one of our vintage rifles. The shot ricocheted around between two panzer tanks and hit one of the Arabs in the back of the head, causing instant death.

At this stage of the private war any talking by our ships company was in any language but English. We retreated back to the upper deck and after hoisting the German Ensign on No.130 we pushed off and found a quieter wreck to secure to for the rest of the night.

After an uneventful dash during the early hours we made St Elmo's Breakwater at daybreak and were badly shaken to learn that our fighter escort for a little while was German, not English!

We were by R/T directed into Sliema creek which was H/Q of Captain (S) Subs. Malta. From memory this was a Commander G.R. Simpson RN, who ordered my ship's company to "abandon ship and get into the air raid shelter, forget about tying up, forget about your SPs/SBs, get ashore, there are only the Quick and the Dead here. Welcome to Malta!"

We survived, and in the course of the next few days it dawned on the 'Powers that Be', that there was no 87 Octane fuel on the island, so we were stuck. They had heard we ran on diesel fuel, hence ATBNFU.

Eventually two of the River Class Submarines brought in our fuel in their ballast tanks; one arrived from Alexandria and the other from Gibraltar. We used the air line pressure system of the Subs to repeatedly blow out our upper deck tanks. We then filled them with soapy water and again blew them out: they still made a wonderful display when stitched with German Incendiaries!

Now we had the fuel and could operate, so we set up base in M'sida Creek, opposite the torpedo depot. Our mooring was alongside a couple of waterlogged barges and our HQ was a building with a wonderful garden and called St Michaels, next to a large block of flats called "Whitehall". We officers were adopted by Lt/Col Ellis and family and we shared their air raid shelter until we disappeared. Lt/Col Ellis was VC Internal Broadcasting on the island and this in the main was for air raid alerts. Our people were able to listen into German and Italian R/ T. Around the island we had flagpoles in many separate areas, by day a Red Flag would be hoisted when we heard we were on the point of an attack and by night a red light would be switched on. I believe that on quite a few occasions the time that elapsed between warning and the all clear amounted to WEEKS, not just hours or days.

Once we were operational our duties, mainly at night were to meet and escort our submarines in and out of the harbour via the swept channel. A one off operation covering several horrendous journeys through the minefields, under the cover of darkness, was to tow a barge to the wreck of HMS *Breckonshire* lying upside down in Marsaxlokk Bay, on the south end of the island, and attempt to cut holes in her bottom and hand pump out any oils etc that we could.

I think the enemy were tipped off about our nightly excursions because we were repeatedly attacked whilst lying alongside the wreck, even though it was dark. With the hull being hit so often the operation was abandoned.

I also remember an incident that occurred after an air raid. As we left our dugout I observed that the masts on the ML had disappeared. On looking around I observed a large hole in the big door near us and on closer inspection found that a bomb had gone through it and had not exploded. It would appear that the bomb had bounced on the water, flown over the boat, taking with it the masts, and gone on through the door!

Our term of office in Malta was ended on the night of the 5/6th May 1942 and again we feel that the enemy were tipped off. The day started with an MOI camera team on the island for a few days to see and record Malta in action and they had no luck with the Air Force being unable to do dummy runs and the Army not prepared to waste valuable ammunition in showing off for films.

HML 130 was duty boat and had to represent the Navy in action. This entailed lots of manoeuvres from alongside and without the protection of camouflage nets, all being repeated time and time again with cameras on the shore and again on board both for and aft. This fiasco lasted until the warning was sounded and everybody withdrew to the "comfort" of the shelters. The raids lasted all day and seemed to centre on M'sida Creek. However, come nightfall we had to escort two Subs out to sea and go about their business, so we turned round and headed back towards St Elmo Breakwater and were approximately a mile off when we were illuminated by shore searchlights from at least four points.

We were completely blinded by these lights (I can still feel the heat of those lights, they were so close). The Army had in fact picked up enemy E-Boats and were trying to draw my attention to them, but unfortunately we were blind. The "E" Boats had tailed us in along the swept channel even though we did a zig-zag course. In the ensuing fight the 115ft long Fairmile "B" ML (built of ¾ inch thick Ply, double skinned and fuelled by 87 Octane spirit) was shattered and eventually burnt down to the waterline and sunk, approximately three quarters of a mile SE of St Elmo Breakwater. The "E" Boats, of steel construction and running on diesel, suffered the following losses:[5] one boat sunk, one abandoned and sunk and one written off after running out of control entering Augusta Harbour through damage received in action. Our losses were the Boat, HMML 130, 4 men killed, 8 men severely wounded and one bloke got away without a scratch. All survivors were picked up by "E "Boats and at first treated in hospital at Augusta by the Italians and later taken to a German hospital at Catania.

After a couple of months when all were fit we were transferred by train to Germany and then to an Interrogation Centre called Oberusal, just north of Frankfurt. Several weeks later we were transferred to the main Naval Camp at Westertimke, called *Marlag U Milag Nord*, roughly halfway between Hamburg and Bremen, nearest town Zevern. There we remained as guests of Hitler for the rest of the war (3 years). Upon being released we returned home, had a few months leave, and then returned to duty.

---

[5] Gained from Kriegsmarine H.Q. at Bremerhaven at the end of the war and being the official German Narrative.

THIS CREST OF THE "CHESHIRE REGIMENT" WAS UNVEILED BY Mrs. MACKENZIE, WIFE OF REAR ADMIRAL KENNETH H.L. MACKENZIE, C.B.E. ADMIRAL SUPERINTENDENT, ON THE 17TH FEBRUARY, 1943, TO CEMENT THE HAPPY ASSOCIATION BETWEEN H.M. DOCKYARD, MALTA, AND THE 1ST BATTALION OF THE CHESHIRE REGIMENT.

THE REGIMENT WAS RESPONSIBLE FOR THE DEFENCE OF THE DOCKYARD FROM 15TH APRIL 1941 - 23RD JANUARY, 1943. DURING THIS PERIOD THE ISLAND RECEIVED 2710 AIR ALERTS, OF WHICH 119 BOMBING ATTACKS WERE CONCENTRATED ON THE DOCKYARD, AN ESTIMATED AGGREGATE OF 700 TONS OF BOMBS BEING DROPPED IN THIS AREA "B" COMPANY OF THE BATTALION WAS STATIONED IN THE DOCKYARD, AND THEIR QUARTERS WERE FOUR TIMES DESTROYED BY DIRECT HITS.

THE BATTALION DISTINGUISHED ITSELF BY SUCCESSFULLY UNLOADING S.S. "PAMPAS" WHILST SUBJECTED TO CONTINUOUS ENEMY BOMBING, THE VESSEL BECOMING A TOTAL WRECK. ON ANOTHER OCCASION THEY ASSISTED H.M.S. "PENELOPE" TO GET TO SEA BY HELPING TO SUPPLY AMMUNITION TO HER DURING HEAVY ENEMY BOMBING, HER AMMUNITION HAVING BEEN EXHAUSTED OWING TO HER ANTI-AIRCRAFT WEAPONS BEING IN CONTINUOUS ACTION.

THUS THE 1ST BATTALION THE 22ND (CHESHIRE) REGIMENT SHARED WITH THE DOCKYARD PERSONNEL THE RIGOURS OF THE SECOND SIEGE OF MALTA.

The Cheshire Regiment Crest

Station Sick Quarters, Takali. 1942.

This was the third direct hit in March 1942. After the second, which landed in the room next to where Flt Lt Bill Gibson was taking morning sick parade, Bill had a chat with Sergeant Harris. During the next week a first aid post was established in a nearby quarry. Although it was in the dispersal area of the Spitfires, Bill convinced the executive that it was much safer than the Mansion house, which stood out like a sore thumb. Bill, the hygiene staff and the whole medical staff built the blast wall themselves. The local Army unit provided the water and telephone, and candles did for light. The blast wall later withstood a 500-pound bomb which landed just 10 paces away.

The new Station Sick Quarters in the quarry, complete with blast wall.

Station Sick Quarters staff, RAF Takali, 1942.

Spitfire on the deck of USS *Wasp*. HMS Eagle in background.

HMS Jervis, Alexandria, 1942.

MV Pampas, raised from the dead, Toxteth dock, Liverpool, early 1950s.
She served in the March 1942 convoy to Malta and was shelled by a battleship but not hit and was the first ship to enter the Grand Harbour.

General Gort.

Reta Barker with dancers at the John Ball Music Hall.

Party at Farson's Brewery.

Jack Allen, 39 Squadron Beaufort pilot, Malta 1943.
Jack was a pianist with Joe Loss's band before the war.

Troops disembarking from SS Port Chalmers. Ran Nestor.

Survivors leaving ship by LST.

Three anti-aircraft guns presented to Malta by Stan Frazer.
Now located at Luqa.

The price of war.

Rock shelter at Mtarfa.

Scenes of destruction in Valetta, 1942.